I WAS WRONG

I WAS WRONG

DENNIS PRINCE

CREATION
HOUSE

I Was Wrong by Dennis Prince
Published by Creation House
A Charisma Media Company
600 Rinehart Road
Lake Mary, Florida 32746
www.charismamedia.com

All scripture quotations, unless otherwise stated, are from the Holy Bible, New International Version. Copyright © 1973, 1978, 1984, 2010, 2011, International Bible Society. Used by permission.

Scripture quotations marked NIV1984 are from the Holy Bible, New International Version. Copyright © 1973, 1978, 1984, International Bible Society. Used by permission.

Scripture quotations marked NKJV are from the New King James Version of the Bible. Copyright © 1979, 1980, 1982 by Thomas Nelson, Inc., publishers. Used by permission.

Some names have been changed in the book to protect the privacy of the persons concerned.

Design Director: Bill Johnson
Cover design by Nathan Morgan

Visit the author's website: www.iwaswrongthebook.com

Library of Congress Cataloging-in-Publication Data: 2013937677
International Standard Book Number: 978-1-62136-363-7
E-book International Standard Book Number: 978-1-62136-364-4

While the author has made every effort to provide accurate telephone numbers and Internet addresses at the time of publication, neither

First edition

13 14 15 16 17 — 9 8 7 6 5 4 3 2 1
Printed in the United States of America

TABLE OF CONTENTS

Introduction xiii

Section 1: Atheists xv

    1: *The Atheist Philosopher* 1

    2: *The Honest Atheist* 6

    3: *The Atheist and the Salvos* 10

    4: *The Marxist Atheist* 12

Section 2: Facts 17

    5: *The Scientists* 19

    6: *Did Jesus Exist?* 24

    7: *The All-Time Number One Best-Selling Book* 28

    8: *The Bible Mistakes* 30

Section 3: Miracles 33

    9: *The Miracle* 35

    10: *God and Suffering* 38

    11: *The Rebellious Son* 41

    12: *The Guilt-Ridden Crim* 44

    13: *The Giver* 48

    14: *The Gaming Addict* 50

    15: *The Desperate Couple* 72

    16: *God and Sex* 76

    17: *The Gay* 86

Section 4: Heaven 97

    18: The Boy Who Went to Heaven 99

    19: The Disabled Son 103

    20: The Songwriter 107

    21: The Future 111

Section 5: Religion 113

    22: The Hindu Guru 115

    23: The Muslim 123

    24: Christian Evil 136

Section 6: Wind-Up 139

    25: My Stories 141

    26: When Teacher Stepped Out 147

    27: Outro 152

    28: The Power Source 155

    29: The Greatest Love of All 161

Notes 165

About the Author 170

Contact the Author 171

By the Same Author 172

My message and my preaching were not with wise and persuasive words, but with a demonstration of the Spirit's power, *so that your faith might not rest on human wisdom, but on God's power.*

—1 Corinthians 2:4–5, emphasis added

DEDICATION

To our three children,
and their sensational spouses,
and our eleven grandchildren.
They have taken the baton and run with it.
Pretty to watch.

INTRODUCTION

Iɴ 2012, ᴀ Global Atheist Convention took take place in my city—Melbourne, Australia. On learning about the convention, something leapt inside me, and I felt compelled to respond. I produced a twelve-page newspaper, *The Regal Standard*, for churches to distribute. Incredibly eighty thousand copies sold, and people were clamoring for more even after the convention was over! Clearly there was a hunger in people to learn more about the atheist movement and how to respond to it, so I decided to expand the content of the newspaper into a book.

I believe what made *The Regal Standard* successful lay in its different approach. Most "answers for atheists" literature has a philosophical bent, or rational emphasis, relying on reason to prove God's existence. That's only part of the story. Certainly God is rational, and rational thinking can lead the honest seeker to God. But there is another aspect of God that is much neglected in debate: the experiential.

God's existence is revealed not only by what He said and did in the past, but by things He *still* says and does. The Bible says God confirms the truth of His message "by signs, wonders and various miracles, and by gifts of the Holy Spirit" (Heb. 2:4). The Bible is full of examples of divine interventions in the lives of mankind, and even after two thousand years that has not changed! "Signs, wonders, and miracles" still serve as ongoing evidences of God's existence and character. Merely possessing a philosophical knowledge of God is not the only portion of the believing Christian; they have access to a dynamic spiritual experience, and millions tell of countless divine interventions as they walk with God.

Philosophies about God inevitably spark debate, where complex issues and persuasive arguments can sometimes cloud the truth about God. But when a miracle stares you in the face, He is not so easily explained away. I have canvassed this book with stories of diverse, remarkable, wonderful God interventions in the lives of men and women for this very reason. These divine interventions reveal the breathtaking, creative diversity of God. He is original. He is His own master. He does things His way, which is beyond our limited understanding set within the context of our world's rules.

Having promised a non-philosophical book, I should say a few stories do have a philosophical stamp. The opening article is one of these—an atheistic philosopher who changed his view. The article is important because it exposes weaknesses in rational analysis, opening the door to the "God-at-work" chapters. A few other chapters answer some of the common questions people ask when confronted with the reality of God.

The stories here might be remarkable, but they are not exceptional. I recently had dinner with friends and, as Christians do, we swapped miracle stories. The God stories were plentiful, and some so extraordinary, so breathtaking, it would cheapen them to put them in print. The stories you are about to read happen all the time.

So I challenge you to read on with an open mind and heart, believe, and give honor to God.

BLESS YOU,

DENNIS PRINCE

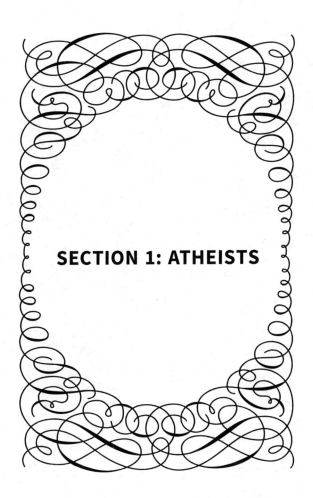

SECTION 1: ATHEISTS

Chapter 1
THE ATHEIST PHILOSOPHER
Why the World's Most Notorious Atheist Called It Quits

H E WAS A philosophical heavyweight, the golden boy of atheism. He had led the field in atheistic thinking and in debates against believers. Then one day he took the podium and announced he got it wrong. What happened?

Professor Antony Flew was not your everyday run-of-the-mill atheist. Amongst his academic allies, he was renowned for his groundbreaking approach to atheistic thinking, which helped set the atheist agenda for fifty years. But in a giant turnaround, he methodically abandoned all his ideas, confessing all in his book *There Is a God.* "A relic from the past" is how he describes one of his former theories.[1]

It's not as though Flew had been wishy-washy in his atheistic dogmas. In debates with Christians he had said things such as, "I know there is no God," and, "A system of belief about God...contains the same...sort of contradictions as unmarried husbands or round squares."[2]

And his influence on atheistic thinking was not trifling. One of his atheistic papers, "Theology and Falsification," was the most widely reprinted philosophy publication of the last century. One leading atheist called it "a classic in the philosophy of religion."

What kind of person was Flew? Paradoxically, he came from a strong Christian home—his father a leading Wesleyan Methodist minister. But the Nazi treatment of Jews he witnessed prior to World War II unsettled his faith. "How can there be evil if God is good?" he questioned. Later he observed, "I reached the conclusion about the nonexistence of God much too quickly, much too easily and for what later seemed to me the wrong reasons."[3]

But a seed thought planted in his youth eventually germinated and became a tree that would overwhelm Flew's skepticism. That seed was a simple principle of Socrates: "Follow the argument

1

wherever it leads." This became his guiding star, and he subjected atheism (and every philosophy) to it. So, when he came across conclusive evidence pointing to the existence of God, he could comfortably make the change. He was still operating within his belief system—follow the argument wherever it leads. To Flew, it was simple honesty.

In May 2004, while attending one of his many public debates against Christians at New York University, he announced his backflip to a stunned audience. He now accepted the existence of a God. The evening became, as he said in typical philosophy jargon, a "joint exploration of the developments in modern science that seemed to point to a higher Intelligence."[4]

One big factor in Flew's U-turn was the complexity of the DNA (see below), but more evidence was needed. Over the years he had built many formidable arguments against the existence of God, and every one had to be dismantled. So, in *There Is a God*, he trawls through all his old ideas, explaining how new information or understanding had demolished each one until he had no more ground to stand on.

He boils them down to three key issues: laws of nature, the universe, and life. He asks where they came from, and then explains what he found.

For the *laws of nature* (i.e., Newton's laws, Boyle's law, etc.) Flew quotes famous scientists—both premodern (e.g., Newton and Maxwell) and recent (e.g., Stephen Hawking and Einstein). All of them, he observes, expressed wonder at the mystery and origin of the laws of nature, and either hinted (or concluded) that God must be behind them. "Compelling and irrefutable," Flew concludes.[5]

On the *existence of life*, Flew asks: How can mindless matter produce living beings who:

- Are purpose driven?
- Can reproduce?
- Have inbuilt coded chemistry (DNA)?

Flew is aware of scientific evolutionary theories that propose how life first arose. But, he says, these theories deal only with interaction of chemicals. They explain nothing of the purpose driven and coding issues essential to living beings. Unless these issues are satisfactorily addressed, he is unconvinced.

On the *existence of the universe*, Flew says the big bang theory changed everything. Before the big bang theory, it seemed the universe had no starting point; it had existed forever and, therefore, didn't need a Creator. But suddenly Flew was confronted with a starting point and the question, "What caused it?" Genesis 1:1 reared its head: "In the beginning God created the heavens and the earth." He concluded, "the universe is something that begs an explanation."[6]

Finally, he reasons, "There are no good philosophical reasons for denying God to be the explanation of the universe."[7]

He insists his discovery was a "pilgrimage of reason," not a step of faith. But it led him, he says, to a God who is self-existent, unchanging, immaterial (a spirit—not made of matter), omnipotent (all-powerful), and omniscient (all-knowing)—a God he says was best fitted by the God of the Judeo-Christian faith.

Oddly, Flew confesses that while he believes God exists, he has no personal experience of God. He simply says, "Christianity is the one religion that most clearly deserves to be honored and respected,"[8] and "No other religion enjoys anything like the combination of a charismatic figure like Jesus and a first-class intellectual like St. Paul. If you're wanting omnipotence to set up a religion, it seems to me that this is the one to beat!"[9]

The book finishes with a section by Flew's biographer, Roy Varghese. This section is a critical appraisal of five prominent atheists, exposing their basic errors. An article about the fundamentals of the Christian faith, written by a close friend of Flew, New Testament scholar N.T. Wright, rounds out the book. Flew says Wright's article is "by far the best case for accepting Christian belief that I have ever seen."[10]

After reading a heavy book like this, you feel grateful that we all don't have to suffer decades of philosophical struggling to discover there is a God. Half a glance at creation is more than enough. Believe and enjoy.

DNA Means "Definitely No Atheism"

The "almost unbelievable complexity" of DNA convinced Flew that intelligence must have been involved. Commenting on one of his Christian debaters, Flew says, "I was particularly impressed with Gerry Schroeder's...refutation of what I call the 'monkey theorem.' This idea...defends the possibility of life arising by chance using the analogy of a multitude of monkeys banging away on computer keyboards and eventually ending up writing a Shakespearean sonnet."[11] That being the case, and given enough time (billions of years), matter could combine in the right form and with its complex DNA to produce life.

Schroeder did his sums. He chose the Shakespearean sonnet that begins, "Shall I compare thee to a summer's day..." containing 488 letters.

Then he calculated the chances of the monkeys hitting the first letter "S"—this is one chance in twenty-six (there are twenty-six letters in the alphabet); the chance of hitting the first two letters "Sh"—is 1 in 26 x 26; the chance of hitting the first three letters "Sha"—is 1 in 26 x 26 x 26, etc. For the whole 488 letters the chances are 1 in 26^{488}—or 1 in 10^{690}.

To give a feel for the magnitude of 10^{690}, Schroeder compared the number of protons, electrons, and neutrons in the *universe*. There are "only" 10^{80}! So, the number 10^{690} is incredibly—and ridiculously—vast.

Bottom line? If the chance of monkeys typing out a sonnet is 1 in 10^{690} (meaning the odds are effectively impossible), then the chance of life arising spontaneously, with the intricacies of the DNA (*far* more complex than a Shakespearean sonnet), are effectively nil.

So life didn't simply "happen"; there was an intelligent Designer. Flew found this reasoning totally convincing.

For a more recent challenge to the idea that life came into existence through naturalistic means, see *Mind and Cosmos: Why the Materialist Neo-Darwinian Conception of Nature Is Almost Certainly False.* The author is respected philosopher Thomas Nagel of New York University. Author of numerous books and papers on philosophy, he is creating waves with this volume. Though still a confirmed atheist, he calls the prevailing scientific view of origins "a heroic triumph of ideological theory over common sense," something he believes will "seem laughable in a generation or two."[12]

The book is honest and courageous. Nagel observes that his views, "will strike many people as outrageous, but that is because almost everyone in our secular culture has been browbeaten into regarding the reductive research program [i.e., life emerged by naturalistic means] as sacrosanct, on the grounds that anything else would not be science."[13]

Unfortunately, this is a book for academics; however, if you are comfortable with words such as: "connotative," "phenomenological," "protomental," "monism," "panpsychism," and "genotypic"; and phrases such as: "nepotistic interpretation of innate altruistic dispositions," you may find it a breeze to read.

That's how Professor Flew discovered God really does exist. It was hard work, but he got there! Next is another example where an atheist academic takes an honest look at evidence of a different kind and reluctantly reaches a "God" conclusion.

Chapter 2
THE HONEST ATHEIST

"As an atheist, I truly believe Africa needs God"

A REMARKABLE ARTICLE APPEARED in *The Times* December 2008, titled, "As an atheist, I truly believe Africa needs God." It was subtitled, "Missionaries, not aid money, are the solution to Africa's biggest problem—the crushing passivity of the people's mindset."

The author, Matthew Parris, was a UK Conservative Member of Parliament from 1979 to 1986. He has written many books on politics and travel; in 2005, he won the Orwell prize for journalism.

The following is an excerpt of the *Creation* magazine article, "Atheists credit the Gospel":

> Parris' [revealing] article was written from a very personal perspective, dwelling particularly on his experience in various countries in Africa during his childhood, and during an extensive tour across the continent when in his twenties. Of a more recent visit to see a village well development project, he wrote:
>
> "It inspired me, renewing my flagging faith in development charities. But travelling in Malawi refreshed another belief, too: one I've been trying to banish all my life, but an observation I've been unable to avoid since my African childhood. It confounds my ideological beliefs, stubbornly refuses to fit my worldview, and has embarrassed my growing belief that there is no God.
>
> "Now a confirmed atheist, I've become convinced of the enormous contribution that Christian evangelism makes in Africa: sharply distinct from the work of secular NGOs, government projects and international aid efforts. These alone will not do. In Africa Christianity changes people's hearts. It brings a spiritual transformation. The rebirth is real. The change is good."

Rebirth? Spiritual transformation? Hardly the language of an atheist. But nevertheless, Parris' atheism is real. He tells of trying to "avoid this truth" of what he was observing, wanting to applaud the practical work of the [missionary] churches while ignoring other aspects of missionary work. "It's a pity, I would say, that salvation is part of the package," writes Parris, "but Christians black and white, working in Africa, do heal the sick, do teach people to read and write; and only the severest kind of secularist could see a mission hospital or school and say the world would be better without it. I would allow that if faith was needed to motivate missionaries to help, then, fine: but what counted was the help, not the faith."

However, as Parris admitted, "this doesn't fit the facts." He explained how Christian faith benefits the poor not merely because of its supportive effect on the missionary, but because "it is also transferred to his flock. This is the effect that matters so immensely, and which I cannot help observing."

Parris notes indeed what many other people, past and present, have observed in those who believe the Gospel. "The Christians were always different. Far from having cowed or confined its converts, their faith appeared to have liberated and relaxed them."

Matthew Parris also notes that Christians had a certain "liveliness, a curiosity, an engagement with the world—a directness in their dealings with others" that was lacking in non-believers. "They stood tall," he writes.

Recalling his driving tour in a Land Rover with four student friends when he was aged 24, Parris observed that the difference between Christians and non-Christians was particularly striking in "lawless" parts of the sub-Sahara. "Whenever we entered a territory worked by missionaries, we had to acknowledge that something changed in the faces of the people we passed and spoke to: something in their eyes, the way they approached you direct, man-to-man, without looking down or away. They had not become more deferential towards strangers—in some ways less so—but more open."

His recent trip to see the village development project in Malawi brought him in close contact with charity workers. Although Parris admits that it would suit him to believe that their "honesty, diligence and optimism in their work" had no connection with their evident personal faith, he had to concede that they were undeniably "influenced by a conception of man's place in the Universe that Christianity had taught."

Parris also makes this astute observation: "There's long been a fashion among Western academic sociologists for placing tribal value systems within a ring fence, beyond critiques founded in our own culture: 'theirs' and therefore best for 'them'; authentic and of intrinsically equal worth to ours.

"I don't follow this. I observe that tribal belief is no more peaceable than ours; and that it suppresses individuality." He goes on to say that such a mindset "feeds into the 'big man' and gangster politics of the African city: the exaggerated respect for a swaggering leader" and does nothing to allay fear of evil spirits, ancestors and nature that so burden many in Africa. Parris writes that "a great weight grinds down the individual spirit, stunting curiosity. People won't take the initiative, won't take things into their own hands or on their own shoulders."

But in stark contrast, Christianity, "with its teaching of a direct, personal, two-way link between the individual and God, unmediated by the collective, and unsubordinate to any other human being, smashes straight through the philosophical/spiritual framework I've just described. It offers something to hold on to for those anxious to cast off a crushing tribal groupthink. That is why and how it liberates."

Parris concludes by warning that aid programs that focus only on provision of material supplies and technical knowledge are unlikely to succeed. "Removing Christian evangelism from the African equation may leave the continent at the mercy of a malign fusion of Nike, the witch doctor, the mobile phone and the machete."[1]

From a convinced atheist that is a stunning reflection—that Christian missionaries (in other words, "Jesus") are the answer to "Africa's biggest problem—the crushing passivity of the people's mindset." You could almost rest the case here! But there is more.

Here is another atheist's honest acknowledgement of something he can't explain—God at work in the lives of ordinary men and women.

Chapter 3
THE ATHEIST AND THE SALVOS
The "Religious Impulse"

ALTHOUGH AN ATHEIST, veteran British politician Roy Hattersley is [surprisingly] considered something of an authority on the origins of the Salvation Army, since he wrote a best-selling biography of [the founders] William and Catherine Booth.

Hence it wasn't too surprising that a BBC program [in January 2010] about the Salvation Army's effectiveness sought his opinion on the subject. The narrator, Peter Day, put it to Hattersley that, "This sort of thing, a sort of social entrepreneurial drive which starts off out of a particular place and circumstances—those sorts of things often run out of steam after a generation or two. Is the Salvation Army in danger of running out of steam?"[1]

Hattersley's response was immediate and effusive:

"I don't think the Salvation Army is remotely in danger of running out of steam. And I think it remains a vibrant organization because of its convictions. I'm an atheist. But I can only look with amazement at the devotion of the Salvation Army workers. I've been out with them on the streets and seen the way they work amongst the people, the most deprived and disadvantaged and sometimes pretty repugnant characters. I don't believe they would do that were it not for the religious impulse. And I often say I never hear of atheist organizations taking food to the poor. You don't hear of "Atheist Aid" rather like Christian aid, and, I think, despite my inability to believe myself, I'm deeply impressed by what belief does for people like the Salvation Army."[2]

So here are two stories of convinced atheists who graciously acknowledged the effectiveness of the Christian gospel in areas they knew well. It is remarkable that atheists, after witnessing activities like that, don't get on board and enjoy the treasures of the faith. Do any of them ever escape their skepticism? What does it take to move an atheist? Take a look at this next story.

Chapter 4
THE MARXIST ATHEIST
What Does It Take to Persuade One?

T HE LAST TWO stories demonstrated how atheists came to the conclusion of God's existence merely by debunking some of the very theories that atheism supports. Now I share with you the testimony of a former Marxist atheist who had a supernatural experience with God and was forever changed. Today, Peter McHugh serves as senior pastor of the Stairway Church in Melbourne, Australia.

The following is a transcript of a testimonial he gave at *Undeniable*, a response event to the Global Atheist Convention, held at Federation Square in Melbourne, on Sunday, April 15, 2012, with several thousand people in attendance:

> Good evening everybody. My name's Peter and it's just great to be with you tonight.
>
> I'm a social worker by training. I've worked with people all my life and I know that in our quiet moments we all wonder: is there something beyond this life, is there something after death?
>
> Now, you know there's a bunch of people who don't believe that's the case. I used to be one of those myself. Knowledge is built on ideas and experience, and growing up in a religious background, my experience of God was rules and regulations. He wanted to beat you up. He thought we were all hopeless and He just wanted to be angry with us. So, I got into my teenage years and started to think about life and what it's all about, and my experience took me into ideas. By the time I got to university I didn't believe in God. I thought He was just a waste of space. I became a Marxist student politician who believed that Christians were nerds, that religion was an opiate for the masses. So at Sydney University I would sit on the lawns and wait for Christians to come to me and

have an argument with them (much like some people up the back having arguments right now!). The whole debate was my ideas engaging with their experience.

And that's what it's like here tonight. We can have ideas about God, but when you experience him, everything changes.

So as an atheist, I had ideas that were built on my experience, my childhood experience of religion. And I'd argue with Christians, and they'd always get to this point. I got really frustrated with them because they'd get to a place of experience and they'd jump across this chasm called faith and just say, "Well, we just believe." And I'd say "come back here, have the argument with me, be logical." And they wouldn't come back over the chasm. They wanted to stay on the side of "we have had an experience." And that's really difficult to argue with, when someone tells you [his] story like that.

And so I got my life into a bit of a mess, and found myself beginning to ask some of the deeper questions. When I was over in Adelaide watching the West Indies thump Australia in the cricket I had a phone call from a Sydney friend who invited me to come to church. So I thought, well, life's a bit meaningless at the moment, and I went along and hung out with him at church—the morning service. I thought I'd walked onto the set of a Blues Brothers movie. It was a crazy Pentecostal church. I wasn't used to that at all and thought "Wow! This is very unusual!" And so I went again that night and I was sitting there listening to it and, you know, I was having an experience that I didn't really realize was going on.

Now when you go to some churches they ask you the question, "Do you want to become a Christian? Do you want to give your life to Jesus? If so put up your hand." And so, I'm sitting there—my head's saying, "Religion's an opiate for the masses. This is all a crock. This is nonsense." And my hand went up in the air. So as an atheist, I looked at my hand and I pulled it down. And then my other hand went up in the air. And so I pulled it down.

Then, if you've been to a church like this, they next say "If you raised your hand, come out the front." Now my head is saying, "I'm not going out the front" as I'm literally walking out the front. And so, I get out the front. It's a Pentecostal church—you know, Blues Brothers movie—and in those churches when they pray for people they sometimes fall over.

"They had to be touching a nerve on the back of his neck or they were pushing him over or something," the atheist in me said. So I figured out—I knew enough from my university—that if I got the center of gravity in my favor, he couldn't push me over.

I prayed something—I don't know what it was I prayed—know that I asked to be forgiven. And the guy that was there, he didn't get any closer than the edge of the stage to me and I fell flat on my back. I cried for an hour. I had an encounter with God.

So here tonight, I can still tell you every reason why you should not be a Christian, I still know all those arguments; they are still well and truly in my head. But those arguments mean nothing because I've had an experience with God.

So, knowledge is based on ideas and experience and at the end of the day, what we're trying to say here tonight is that experience will ultimately trump ideas. And that's the frustrating thing about Christians and if you're here tonight and you don't have faith in Jesus and you are in an atheist position or another alternative belief system, we're not trying to convince you that we're right, we're just telling you that we've had an experience that has changed our lives and we're inviting you to consider whether that might work for you. If it's not going to work for you, then that's cool, that's great; that's entirely up to you.

But we know that Jesus Christ is real because of experience, not just ideas in our head.[1]

"I fell flat on my back. I cried for an hour. I had an encounter with God."

Experiences like that are hard to explain rationally; they bother us. We want the facts; we want to Google them; we want to find out from a scientist, understand what's going on and get the issues under control. So what does the scientist say? How do such people explain God? This next section deals with some facts, beginning with three scientists and their views.

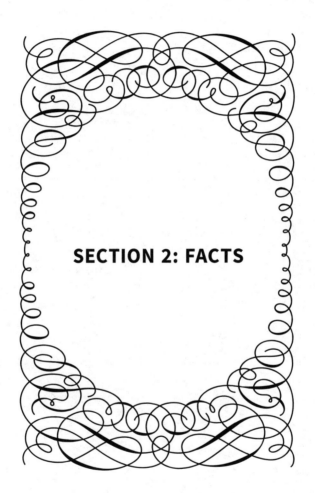

SECTION 2: FACTS

Chapter 5
THE SCIENTISTS

You Can Trust a Scientist; Let's Hear What They Say

God and science are compatible. That's the message according to a growing number of scientists. It seems scientists are discovering that the more they learn about science, the more they see the hand of a Designer—not evolution—is responsible for all we see around us.

Lots of people would be surprised to learn that many scientists not only have no problem when it comes to believing in God, they say it even helps them in their work! The scientists making this discovery are not lackeys. Their CVs are almost as long as the technical papers they write.

Following are the brief biographies of three scientists and their CVs and some of their work and philosophy. It's worth adding that there was not a problem finding scientists like these; the problem was deciding which ones to leave out.

Dr. Richard Smalley

Dr. Richard Smalley (1943—2005), MA, PhD (Princeton) was the Hackerman Professor of Chemistry, Physics, and Astronomy at Rice University. He was awarded the Nobel Prize in Chemistry in 1966 for his discovery of (and research on) a totally new allotrope (form) of carbon. This comprised unique soccer-ball-shaped molecules he called buckminsterfullerenes, which he nicknamed *buckyballs*.[1] Many researchers date the dawn of modern nanotechnology to this discovery. For his contributions and research, he was also awarded eight honorary doctor of science degrees.

Skeptical of religion for most of his life, Dr. Smalley became a Christian in his last years, partly due to his intensive study of Intelligent Design.

At first he struggled with the idea that science was compatible with Christianity. But, challenged by an intelligent design lecture at his university, he agreed to look more closely at evolution. His reaction to what he found was, initially, anger. His wife (a biologist who had yet to come to terms with the same issue) wrote: "I remember him pacing the bedroom floor in anger, saying evolution was bad science. Rick hated bad science worse than anything else. He said if he conducted his research the way that they did, he would never be respected in the scientific community."[2]

Initially Dr. Smalley embraced theistic evolution—the idea that God worked side by side with evolution. But as he studied in detail, he became an outspoken anti-Darwinist, saying that Darwinian evolution had been given its deathblow with the advance of genetics and cell biology, and it was now clear that biological evolution could not have occurred.[3]

It was during the last year of his life that he made the change from simply believing in God as a creator—or a force—to really trusting Christ to rule his life.[4]

Because of his new Christian understanding he wrote that "the last year of his life was his most thrilling as a scientist. He learned that he did not need to 'throw his mind away when reading the Bible,' but concluded that the Bible made him an even better scientist and a more inspiring science educator."[5]

DR. MATTI LEISOLA

The next scientist, Dr. Matti Leisola, became a Christian in part because of his wife's testimony.

> Dr. Leisola obtained his DSc (Tech) in biotechnology from the Helsinki University of Technology in 1979. His extensive career includes winning the Latsis Prize for a significant young researcher in 1987 in Switzerland, being Director of Research (1988—1997) in an international Biotech company and, most recently, Dean of the Faculty of Chemical and Materials Sciences at the new Finnish Aalto University. He has published over 120 papers, mainly on enzyme research, authored 20 articles in books or conference proceedings, and obtained six patents. Dr. Leisola's scientific articles are cited about 1300 times in the scientific literature.[6]

Dr. Leisola is a passionate Christian, but he wasn't always. He explains:

"I believed the standard story [of evolution] till I was about 22 years old. I used it (as I then thought) as a powerful weapon to argue against the Christian God. Without realizing it, I was a typical product of the western naturalistic educational system and I certainly wanted to remain autonomous, and actually hated the idea of God interfering with my life."

But he changed, thanks to his girlfriend Marja, now his wife:

"She became a Christian and I was suddenly faced with the reality of her changed life and new values. This led me to study the evidence for Christianity. The search led me to Christ. Then I wanted to understand how good a weapon Darwinism was against Christianity, and it did not take much effort to realize that it stood on a shaky foundation. I first realized it when studying biochemistry and the weak efforts to explain the origin of life based on some rudimentary experiments. So it all started with a change in my belief system. Everyone has a belief system and people use their belief system to interpret the facts; it's not really about the facts."[7]

On the issue of Christianity versus science, Dr. Leisola says:

"Christianity is the foundation of modern science and explains why we can do science: a rational God created a rational man in his own image so that he is able to understand the creation with his mind. Indeed, the Creator Jesus Christ is called the Logos (Word—John 1:1–3), and makes sense of this orderly universe and complexity of life. Those believing in a naturalistic explanation for the origin of life are the ones with a blind faith."[8]

DR. STUART BURGESS

Dr. Stuart Burgess, BSc, PhD (Brun), CEng, FlMechE, is Professor of Engineering Design, Department of Mechanical Engineering at the University of Bristol (UK). He is a world expert on biomimetics (imitating design in nature), and leads the Design Engineering

Research Group at his university. Dr. Burgess is the author of over forty papers published in secular science journals, and another fifty-plus conference proceedings. He has also registered seven patents, and is the recipient of a number of prestigious awards for his work.[9]

And he too, is a committed Christian.

One of the projects Dr. Burgess worked on was the hugely expensive Envisat ESA satellite—costing 1.6 billion pounds (sterling), approximately US$2.6 billion.[10]

Dr. Burgess' specialty is biomimetics. He explains why engineers are so interested in this burgeoning field:

> "Biomimetics involves copying or being inspired by design solutions from nature. Engineers are very interested in biomimetics because the natural world contains supremely optimized design. For example, birds and insects are supremely well designed for flight. Birds have inspired aeroplane designers for many years, including the Wright brothers who invented aircraft turning mechanisms after studying how birds turned in the air.
>
> "Flying insects like dragonflies are another strong evidence for design because their flight mechanisms (and navigation systems) are incredibly sophisticated, although evolutionists regard dragonflies as 'primitive' insects that appeared many millions of years ago. My own research group at Bristol University is developing micro air vehicles based on the wings of dragonflies. We have filmed dragonflies with high speed cameras and recorded the exact flapping and twisting motion of their wings. We have then produced linkage mechanisms that can copy that motion in man-made micro air vehicles."[11]

Dr. Burgess is impressed with many designs in the natural world, but one stands out to him:

> "My favourite evidence is the peacock tail feather. It has beautiful iridescent colours produced by thin film interference. The feather has layers of keratin with precision thicknesses comparable to the wavelengths of the individual colours of white light. The feather barbs are also incredibly well aligned

to produce mathematical patterns like ellipsoids and cardioids. The design of peacock feathers is so precise that engineers cannot replicate it. Yet the feathers seem to exist purely for decoration! I think that the peacock feather shows not only that there is a Creator, but that the Creator is supremely wise and very caring. I have no doubt that God wanted humans to enjoy the beauty of the peacock feather."[12]

But he notices reluctance among any scientists to discuss Intelligent Design or the question of the Designer. Some are willing to discuss the subject but are not willing to look any further because of the implications. Because if there is a Creator, they should be accountable to him and give glory and credit to him. That's a stumbling block.

How does Christianity connect with engineering? Dr. Burgess explains:

"Engineering is a great profession for a Christian because it involves creativity. Man's ability to create is one aspect of our being made in the image of God. The difficulty of designing and building things that are relatively simple makes you realize how great is the wisdom and power of God who has made all things."[13]

There are all kinds of other misconceptions about God. One of them even goes so far as to say Jesus never existed. A person who knows God is baffled by doubts like that. It is like someone saying one plus one equals three. Nevertheless, this issue has sown doubts in minds so it needs an answer.

Chapter 6
DID JESUS EXIST?

A THEIST PHILOSOPHER BERTRAND Russell once said during a lecture: "Historically, it is quite doubtful whether Christ ever existed at all, and if He did we do not know anything about Him."[1]

But on another occasion he mused: "I would never die for my beliefs because I might be wrong."[2] Wise words; for on the issue of the existence of Jesus, Russell was simply wrong and should have known better. There are many historical references to Jesus walking this earth and they also tell us quite a lot about Him. In spite of this, Russell and a few like-minded skeptics have influenced a surprisingly large number of people, so we need to examine the facts.

Of course the New Testament provides massive evidence for the existence of Jesus. It is very much a historical book and, on historical issues, it is never faulted, though many have tried. Biblical evidence about people, places, and events have been proven accurate by archaeology time and time again. On the issue of Jesus' existence, skeptics sometimes ignore its evidence on the grounds of bias, but it should not be rejected out of hand. No historians are completely unbiased. Often the best historians have a vested interest in their topic, which is usually why they write about it. Consider the holocaust. The people most interested in recording its atrocities were Jews, yet few question their record of the events. So the Bible should be accepted, alongside all the other ancient records, as a reliable record of Jesus and His activities, and the four Gospels have much information on that.

Nevertheless, for hard-line skeptics it is necessary to compile the evidence from hostile witnesses, people who were not Christians, or were antagonistic to Christianity or were not contributors to the New Testament. We need a good cross section of references from a variety of writers like this, from around the time of Christ. That's a reasonable approach as that's how we know most other historical figures existed.

The following is a list of written references to Jesus made by various historians, writers and identities from the next century after the life of Jesus. (Jesus was born about 4 BC and died about AD 30.)

- In AD 55, the Roman historian Thallus wrote about the darkness that fell at midday when Jesus was crucified. He called it an eclipse, not a miracle. Thallus' original work is lost, but survives through quotations by later historians.[3] Thallus did not doubt Jesus' existence—he was just trying to give a naturalistic explanation for the darkness. (Which was flawed. It was Passover and therefore a full moon, during which an eclipse was not possible.)[4]

- Phlegon wrote a history called *Chronicles*. Although the work is lost, Julius Africanus preserved a section of it in his writings. Phlegon also referred to the darkness that came on the earth at Jesus' crucifixion and, like Thallus, attributes it to an eclipse.[5]

- "Shortly after AD 73, Mara bar Serapion, a Stoic with little known background, wrote a letter to his son describing how the Jews had killed 'their wise king.'"[6]

- "In the AD 90s, the Jewish historian Josephus wrote his second major work, *Antiquities of the Jews*. In it, he described the death of the apostle James, 'the brother of Jesus called Christ.'[7] But consider what his book says before that:
  "'About this time there lived Jesus, a wise man, if indeed one ought to call Him a man. For He was one who wrought surprising feats and was a teacher of such people as accept the truth gladly. He won over many Jews and many of the Greeks. He was the Messiah. When Pilate, upon hearing Him accused by men of the highest standing amongst us, had condemned Him to be crucified, those who had in the first place come to love Him did not give up their affection for Him. On the third day He appeared to them restored to life, for the prophets of God had prophesied these and countless other marvellous things about Him. And the tribe of Christians, so called after Him, has still to this day not disappeared.'"[8]

The references to Jesus as Messiah and his resurrection from the dead are unexpected from a Jew, and some historians believe they were a spurious later addition. Nevertheless many historians acknowledge the rest of the passage as genuine, confirming Jesus' existence.

- "In AD 111, the Roman governor, Pliny the Younger, wrote to Trajan the Emperor regarding administrative matters. His preserved letters represent the largest administrative correspondence to survive from Roman times. In one letter, he asked about the treatment of Christians who are on trial. He derogatorily mentioned Christ three times, and his description of Christian behavior and worship patterns matches much of what we know from the New Testament."[9]

- In AD 116, a well-respected Roman historian, Tacitus, published the *Annals*, a year-by-year history of several Roman emperors. When describing the great fire in Rome in AD 64, he noted the popular theory that 'Chrestians' started the fire.[10] In light of the popular misspelling, he set the record straight: 'Christus, the founder of the name, had undergone the death penalty in the reign of Tiberius, by sentence of the procurator Pontius Pilate.'[11] After this historical footnote, he continued to deride the Christian movement as a 'pernicious superstition.'"[12]

- Suetonius (AD 120), chief secretary to Roman Emperor Hadrian, and contemptuous of Christians, wrote that there was a man named Chrestus (or Christ) who lived during the first century.[13]

- Lucian of Samosata (AD 165) was a second-century Greek writer scornful of Christians. He acknowledges that Jesus was "worshipped by Christians, introduced new teachings, and was crucified for them. He said that Jesus' teachings included the brotherhood of believers, the importance of conversion, and the importance of denying other gods. Christians lived according to Jesus' laws, believed themselves to be immortal, and were characterized by contempt for death, voluntary self-devotion, and renunciation of material goods."[14]

- Celsus (AD 175) attacked Christianity in his writings. These works have not survived but we know of them through the writings of the theologian Origen, who defended Celsus' accusation that Jesus was a magician and a sorcerer.[15]

- "The *Babylonian Talmud* (Sanhedrin 43a) confirms Jesus' crucifixion on the eve of Passover and the accusations against Christ of practicing sorcery and encouraging Jewish apostasy."[16]

- "Then we have all the Gnostic writings (*The Gospel of Truth, The Apocryphon of John, The Gospel of Thomas, The Treatise on Resurrection*, etc.) that all mention Jesus."[17]

The passages are often brief, but that is what you would expect from an era when Romans and Greeks were mainly hostile toward Christians, and Jewish minds were absorbed with the Roman occupation and the destruction of their beloved Jerusalem in AD 70. You would expect only passing references, but references nevertheless that confirmed many of the essential events and activities of Jesus and the faith.

Despite their brevity, the diversity and weight of these references are formidable. Skeptics might haggle over a few, but to write off all of them as spurious is a lost cause. Wikipedia makes the comment: "Virtually all modern scholars of antiquity agree that Jesus existed, and biblical scholars and classical historians regard theories of his non-existence as effectively refuted."[18]

But for the final word we should hear from atheist historian Michael Grant in his book, *Jesus: An Historian's Review of the Gospels*:

> To sum up, modern critical methods fail to support the Christ-myth theory. It has "again and again been answered and annihilated by first rank scholars." In recent years "no serious scholar has ventured to postulate the non-historicity of Jesus"—or at any rate very few, and they have not succeeded in disposing of the much stronger, indeed very abundant, evidence to the contrary.[19]

Chapter 7
THE ALL-TIME NUMBER ONE
BEST-SELLING BOOK

A NOTHER FACT THAT speaks for Jesus' existence is the willingness of many believers, over the course of more than two thousand years, to die, not only for the man Jesus, but also for a copy of His book. Millions have an insatiable desire to scour the pages of the Bible. Statistics for that passion are out there, but they are mostly swept under the carpet. They are a significant indicator of the experience of God we enjoy as a result of knowing the God of the Bible. Look at the numbers:

Top-Selling Books of All Time*	
BOOK	**Millions:**
Bible	6000
Mao's Little Red Book	850
Qur'an	800
Xinhua Dictionary	400
Mao Zedong's articles	252.5
A Tale of Two Cities	200
Scouting For Boys (Baden Powell)	150
Lord of the Rings	150

*Figures for sales of books are approximate. But certainly, as far as the Bible is concerned, there are few who would deny its sales have far outstripped those of every other publication. These figures have been compiled from data on www.publishingperspectives.com and Wikipedia.

The Bible consistently outsells all its competitors. Sales figures are invariably way in front. Figures like these are not fashionable in a media that seeks to be "cool."

Why are Bible sales consistently on top? Because somehow, through the ink on the pages, God reveals Himself to the reader, who finds life, comfort, and help. Six billion Bible owners can't be wrong. For many people it is their most precious possession, and those who live in countries where Bibles are forbidden go to incredible lengths to obtain a copy. Many Christians in free countries help by smuggling them in. It's happening all the time.

The most successful Bible smuggling shipment was conducted by Brother Andrew, author of *God's Smuggler,* in 1981. Funded by donations from around the world, he purchased a tugboat, built a 100-foot submersible barge, printed 232 tons of Bibles (a million copies) and towed them 200 miles up the coast of China, where thousands of Christians were waiting in the dark with bikes, buses, and trucks.

The tug and barge made it safely out of Chinese waters and most Bibles were effectively distributed to grateful believers throughout China. But some of the Christians at the beach were sprung just before the mission was completed. Fishermen saw them and, ignoring pleas from the Christians, informed officials in the nearby village. As a result some of the Bibles and believers were captured. Officials tried to destroy the Bibles, but because they burned so slowly, many were tossed into latrines. But Christians fished them out, washed and dried them and doused them with perfume![1]

When people go to lengths like that you know they found treasure.

That's why the Bible sits securely on the top rung of the listings.

(You can read more about Brother Andrew's mission in *Night of a Million Miracles*, by Paul Estabrooks.)

So millions of people are sold on the Bible and can't get enough of it. But others have problems with it. Can a "Bronze Age" book be trusted? Isn't it full of errors? It's time to address that issue.

Chapter 8
THE BIBLE MISTAKES
Yes, It Has Lots of Them

BELIEVE IT OR not, the Bible is chock full of mistakes. Not one original book of the Bible exists today, and for centuries they were copied by hand. Those copies were copied, and copied again, until the printing press was invented around AD 1440. Copying mistakes were inevitable, so the books of today are not identical to the originals. Therefore, the Bible is unreliable, and we cannot trust it as God's Word.

So goes the common story.

Is it true?

Here are the facts.

The Bible has two parts—Old Testament and New Testament—written over about 1,500 years, the last around AD 97.

For the New Testament, there still exist today 5,656 manuscripts handwritten before the age of printing. It's a simple thing to compare these manuscripts to see if there are differences and mistakes made in copying.

Are there differences? Yes—*many*. It's a fact. Here are some examples.

In Mark 13:33, some manuscripts read, "Be on guard, be alert!" Other manuscripts say, "Be on guard, be alert *and pray!*" (emphasis added).

In Mark 14:24, some manuscripts read, "This is my blood of the covenant..." Other manuscripts say, "This is my blood of the *new* covenant..." (emphasis added).

These are typical of the differences between manuscripts. And it is obvious in these examples that the underlying message is not changed.

Now, while differences are plentiful, they are almost all trivial, like the above. In the few cases where longer passages are uncertain (and for minor issues too), many Bibles have footnotes to show you where manuscripts disagree. The important thing is this: *not one of the differences between manuscripts makes a scrap of difference to any central Christian teaching.* The fundamental Bible message is not affected.

An illuminating comparison can be made with other ancient books. They too have been copied many times over centuries. How reliable are they? Take, for example, Caesar's Gallic Wars, written about 100–44 BC. Only ten handwritten copies exist today, compared with 5,656 for the New Testament. Yet nobody ever dismisses Caesar's Gallic Wars as being unreliable. Not only that, the oldest (and therefore most reliable) of Caesar's Gallic Wars manuscripts was written some one thousand years after the original. Compare this with New Testament manuscripts: some of these were written only about fifty years after the original, most within 150 years!

The point is obvious. The Bible is by far the best-preserved ancient book in the world. We can trust it, because it's God's word to us.

It's one thing to have a wildly popular ancient book about God, but does that prove God is real? Can He reveal His hand and show His power? Better still—fix some of the evil and suffering in the world? Let's look at some miracle stories in this next section.

SECTION 3: MIRACLES

IN THE LAST two sections, I presented anecdotes about atheists who discovered the existence of God by researching for themselves and by the evidence of hard facts. But from this section on, I will present anecdotes and personal stories of people who are proof that miracles do, in fact, exist in the world. The very fact that these miracles took place shouts out the existence of the one true God.

Chapter 9
THE MIRACLE

I T WAS THE most powerful and convincing miracle I have ever personally witnessed. And I was not alone; hundreds watched its progress week by week as people prayed and believed, and God did His work. The lady concerned has since died, gone to a shining reward in heaven, after living a rich and full life thanks to this kindness from God. Here is how it unfolded.

A church in Adelaide, South Australia, was running a healing campaign in a large tent, and I went along with my wife and some friends. A big banner above the stage read: *"I am the Lord that healeth thee*—Exodus 15:26." Beneath it in a wheelchair sat Dianne, a girl in her twenties with an obviously serious disability. It was an incongruous sight—the bold boast of the banner and the terrible disability of the tiny girl. Each seemed to defy the other.

A friend of ours, a nurse, had brought Dianne from her residence—a place called The Home for Incurables (later renamed Julia Farr Centre). At the age of five, Dianne had been diagnosed with a rare bone disease known as polyostotic fibrous dysplasia and had many operations to straighten her legs. She stopped growing at twelve years, at the height of 5'2½" (or approximately 1.33 m). Arthritis had set in, and she developed epilepsy and then severe muscle weakness, and had to be strapped in her chair. She was told she could not bear children, and if she did, they would be spastic or die.

Sometime previously, another nurse had talked to Dianne about God and she had become a committed Christian and even taught Sunday school from her wheelchair.

So here she was sitting through this healing meeting. Afterwards she asked for prayer to be filled with the Holy Spirit. We were waiting on the lawn with other friends of the nurse. I remember saying, "You know I've got faith to believe she can be healed." With her severe condition that was a bold statement, but each one in the group came right back: "So have I!"

Dianne had resisted prayer for healing, believing she was meant to be that way and glorify God in her sick body. But one day she read Acts 28:26–27:

> You will be ever hearing but never understanding; you will be ever seeing but never perceiving. For this people's heart has become calloused; they hardly hear with their ears, and they have closed their eyes. Otherwise they might see with their eyes, hear with their ears, understand with their hearts and turn, and I would heal them.

Convicted by this, Dianne made an appointment with a pastor for healing prayer. After the prayer she asked for her leg plasters to be removed, and she stood up and *walked!* It was a miracle. Her toes were still curled so she asked for prayer for these and they straightened! She then drank from a glass without assistance—she had previously only been able to drink from a baby's bottle!

Two months of strong personal prayer followed, eventually releasing her from epilepsy, fear, and arthritis, and giving her the ability to start a new life. She learned to care for herself and went on to marry and have two children and four grandchildren. Dianne's story was written up in the *Adelaide Advertiser*, the major Adelaide newspaper.

It was a wonderful, indisputable miracle of God. Miracles do happen, just not as often as we would like, thanks to our worldly Western mind-set. Even Jesus was hampered by unbelief. (See Mark 6:1–6.) Nevertheless, practically every Christian can rattle off a few miracles he or she has seen. The happiness enjoyed by Dianne, her husband, her children and grandchildren, and all those who prayed and trusted God for the miracle, is a priceless treasure. We honor God for this great favor and for the myriad of favors He gives every day to His children, all around the world.

It's hard to deny a well-documented miracle like that. Sometimes God intervenes so effectively in the activities of men and women that even the most hardened atheist must acknowledge it. The story is an eye-opener, but it raises questions. Why suffering? Why are people born with disabilities? Why are there tragedies and calamities? Where is God in all this? It's worth looking at before we go on to more miracles.

Chapter 10
GOD AND SUFFERING
Why Doesn't He Do Something?

T HE BABY BORN blind; the terrorist attack; the tsunami; oppression of the innocent—why does God stand by and do nothing? Why doesn't an angel intervene? Why doesn't a bolt from heaven strike the rapist?

There are answers, but they are not simple. They take us back to our origins.

Remember, we are not creatures of time and chance. We were created by God and in His image. There was no evil or suffering in the original world, but that all changed when a man and a woman disobeyed God. Two people chose evil, and the Bible tells us this evil "spread to all men" (Rom. 5:12, NKJV). As a result, the two were banished from God's paradise to an earth that also now suffered from their actions with calamity, death, and misery. You read about this in the first three chapters of Genesis.

Why did God allow Adam and Eve free choice? Why didn't He protect them from their foolishness? Herein lies the heart of the matter. God was building a world in which love could transcend all else and make our home a true paradise. He wanted to love His children extravagantly, and He sought their love in return. But here is the problem: authentic love is not possible unless an authentic choice goes with it—the choice to love or not to love. If we have no such choice, we have no freedom; we are simply robots programmed to act as God decides, unable to give genuine love. No one wants to live like that.

So God was compelled to preserve free choice. A genuine option of evil had to exist, freely accessible, and with potential for all its terrible consequences. Such is the price of love, and God considered it worth it. Love is so profoundly wonderful He took the chance. And that is where we are today—Adam and Eve disobeyed God and we endure the consequences. But note the following.

God could stamp out evil people if He wished. But who would survive? Where would He draw the line? His standard is perfection; none of us would reach that mark, and we have all sinned and caused suffering to others.

And look at this: God has actually fought evil at a huge cost. He allowed His Son Jesus to suffer and die on a cross in our place, for our sin. His plan was to restore us to Himself and help us overcome evil. We can all benefit from this—as we choose. As we embrace the massive benefits He won for us, our own suffering is eased and we are eminently equipped to ease the suffering of others.

God's enemy, Satan, was also given free will, and he too chose evil. He has power, and much disaster and evil is his doing. But again, God has provided believers with a means to deal with Satan's attacks through prayer and spiritual authority. Much evil has been avoided, and much good achieved, through prayer.

We still live, however, with the earthquake, the tsunami, the fire, the flood, and all their dreadful consequences. Sometimes people are miraculously spared, other times they are not. But all who turn to God can find comfort and strength to help in their suffering. There is a power in Scripture and in God's spiritual presence that has helped millions since time began. The Book of Job has been a friend to many.

Nevertheless, there are levels of human suffering that no earthly words can hope to explain. Job was a righteous believer, but in one hour all he owned was swept away. His cries, complaints, and prayers fell on deaf ears, till finally God showed him heaven's glory. A stunned Job repented, saying, "I spoke of things I did not understand" (Job 42:3). A revelation of the splendor and reality of God silences all else. In the end we must trust God's promise "Will not the Judge of all the earth do right?" (Gen. 18:25).

In the age to come, for all who love and follow God, a new earth will be ushered in and everything will be made new: no death, no sorrow, no crying; the last few chapters of the Bible explain it. God, who understands suffering (His own Son was nailed to a cross), has not stood aloof. He has extended Himself utterly, while preserving our free choice, to provide many avenues of help and comfort and, ultimately, an eternal place with Him in paradise.

Back to the miracles: miracles are more plentiful in developing countries. Yes they happen in the West, but developing countries are far more blessed. Why is that? This next story from Dr. Colton Wickramaratne helps us understand why.

Chapter 11
THE REBELLIOUS SON
From Poison to Passion

H E RAISED A ten thousand-strong church in Sri Lanka; delegates from more than eighty countries flock to his conferences; he circles the globe on speaking engagements. But it didn't begin like that.

The bottle of poison was poised over his mouth. Seventeen-year-old Colton Wickramaratne had chosen a neglected botanical garden to end it all, beneath a giant coconut palm close to a stream. "I know there is no God," he said to the sky. "That's why I can't answer all the questions I have. What's the use of living?" But as the crucial moment stared him in the face he wavered and prayed: "God, if You are there...meet me now." Then he saw it—an enormous poster tacked to the tree above him. "If you have come to the end of life's journey and you don't know what to do, remember Jesus Christ is the answer to all of your problems. Come to the YMCA at 6 o'clock."

Astonished that a poster like that would be placed in such a deserted place, he decided to go along. He would create trouble if it was just a lot of nonsense.

It wasn't. A man from Youth for Christ persuaded him to simply be honest. So he prayed desperately, "God if You meet me now, I have nothing to offer You. But I will give You my life."

He described what happened. "The Holy Spirit took over. I felt His presence in a way I could never deny. This was not brainwashing. This was truth. This was power. Suddenly I was sobbing, crying out to God with every fiber of my soul. I could no longer stand in arrogant belligerence...it was like walking from a nightmare into a reassuring new reality."[1]

With that, the young Colton commenced an astonishing new life filled with incredible miracles, all told in his book, *My Adventure in Faith*. Here are just a few.

As Colton was approaching his second year of Bible school, his father died. With his financial support lost and his fees due in three days, he took leave from college to fast and pray. At the end of the three days, no money had come, and he gave up, discouraged. He would just get a job, be a good helper in the church, and give half his income to someone else so they could attend Bible school. But a message called him to the principal, who told him his fees had just been paid by a poor widow in Florida. God had spoken to her and told her to send money for a Bible student in Ceylon (renamed Sri Lanka in 1972). She had no idea even where Ceylon was, but tracked it all down and mailed some cash. (She had to cut back on her own food to do so; and when her bedroom roof leaked, she couldn't afford the repairs, so she slept in the lounge.)

In this way Colton got through Bible school. Ten years later he was able to visit her and express his thanks. She was a feisty lady. A sign in her front yard declared "There is no water in hell." Their story was published in the local paper, and she was proudly taken to church to hear Colton preach.

In 1956, with a baby son and a church of sixty people, Colton became burdened for children and the aimless people around him. For a long time he lost his appetite, couldn't sleep, and wept at the state of his city. One night as he was weeping at his bedside, a hand appeared through a broken windowpane. He switched on the outside light but no one was there. Twice this happened, then he thought it might be God, so he prayed. The hand appeared again, surrounded by a glow, and he saw a nail print. It was Jesus, who began to talk to him, firstly about his pride and priorities. They were attitudes Jesus wanted to correct in his life. Then the window became like a large screen and he saw crowds and eight distinct faces. Jesus told him he would encounter these eight people in the years to come (which he did), and told him many other things. The most striking impression left with Colton was the call to be totally obedient to Christ. He later said, "I believe when it comes to obedience, God will speak to us once or twice. After that He will give that same opportunity to someone else."[2]

One of the people in the vision was a Haitian woman. He remembered kinky hair, wrinkles on her forehead, and a missing toe.

During a visit to Haiti, Colton inquired about such a person, and was driven some distance, followed by a long walk to a round hut with a grass roof. There he met the lady he had seen in his vision. She spoke in Creole; he recognized only one word: "Colton." His translator filled him in. God had told her to pray for a man named Colton from 1957 till she met him. He was amazed. *God works in mysterious ways* was his grateful conclusion.

God told Colton to conduct a conference for Christian leaders in the Third World—he called it *Impetus 80*, with delegates from around fifty-five countries. But a political uprising forced the government to cancel all conferences five days before the event. However, three years before that, Colton had been supernaturally warned of this crisis and was given instructions on how to deal with it. As a result the responsible government minister spoke personally to the president, enabling the conference to go ahead.

Many other remarkable miracles have followed him. His whole life reflects a driving passion to spread the message of Jesus Christ to the whole world, and a willingness to do anything to achieve that goal. He urges people to devote their lives to serving God, saying, "God's method is a man, and you can be that man."[3] At eighty years of age, and frail in body, he is still in demand as a preacher. His message is strident and clear: "Tell someone about Jesus Christ today."

That was a radical transformation of a young man who had been running from God. Here is another radical transformation, this time an older man, Mr. Black. He had also run from God, but for much longer, and when he eventually stopped he found God hard to find. For both these men, their fortunes turned when they stumbled on vibrant Christian gatherings where they paused to listen, then acted.

Chapter 12
THE GUILT-RIDDEN CRIM
By Robyn Kyte

THE FIRST THING my new temporary boss, Mr. Black, said to me was, "Miss Kyte, you are the seventh secretary I have had in six months. Do you, or do you not, intend to stay?" I was taken aback by his aggressive manner but assured him I would stay. However, within two days I determined to leave—the man was so bad-tempered—but someone persuaded me to stay a little longer.

On the second day, during my lunch break, I took my sandwiches and a Bible over to a comfortable chair. Mr. Black came over to ask a question, but then didn't leave. He seemed taken by the Bible on my lap. He began to pace up and down in front of me, making me nervous. Then he swung around and barked: "You know you're saved by grace and not by works lest any man should boast, don't you!" (He was quoting Ephesians 2:8–9.) I was frightened by his forcefulness, but squeaked out, yes, I did know.

Mr. Black said nothing more to me that would make me think he had any religious inclinations, and certainly his behavior didn't show it. His temper was at the surface all the time.

My Christian inclination was to bring people to know Jesus; to do that I would invite them to church. I found out that Mr. Black lived close to my church, so on the first Friday afternoon I nervously approached him and asked if he would like to come with me on Sunday. Of course I expected him to refuse, and be his usual disagreeable self in doing so, but he agreed! He had no transport and asked how he would get there, so I told him I would pick him up.

He sat through the service and we continued sitting there after everyone had filed out. I felt sure Mr. Black would not have liked it. He was a pompous, reserved Englishman who spoke in a refined accent, dressed in finely cut suits, and wore bowler hats. The free-flowing "happy-clappy" Pentecostal service he had just attended would have been very different from the stilted services he might have attended in England. But Mr. Black gave no hint as to his reaction. He merely said, "Hmm, very interesting."

The following week he said nothing to me about the church service, or God, or anything about religion, and continued to be excessively bad-tempered. On Friday afternoon I asked him if he would like to come to church again. He queried, "You'll be organizing transport, Miss Kyte?" I said I would, and so he came.

Next week, once again, he said nothing about church or religion. Despite him being so cross all the time, I had managed to persevere with the job. On the Friday afternoon I said, "Mr. Black, if you're planning on going to church this Sunday, I won't be able to take you, as I have to go somewhere else."

He fired back at me, "Then organize alternative transport for me, Miss Kyte!" So I did.

The next Monday I came in to work, and Mr. Black was working at his desk. Without looking up, he spoke, "Miss Kyte, this baptism in the Holy Spirit. I want it. Organize it for me!"

I laughed and said, "Mr. Black, you can't organize the baptism in the Holy Spirit."

"Just do it!" he retorted.

So I rang my pastor, and he spoke to Mr. Black and arranged for him to come to his house on Saturday afternoon to receive the baptism in the Holy Spirit.

The Sunday morning after this appointment I was driving to Mr. Black's house to pick him up. Not far from his house I was stopped at traffic lights when I noticed him walking toward me. Usually he walked stiff and erect, carrying an umbrella. This time he was swinging the umbrella round and round and singing at the top of his voice! *Mr. Black singing!* I pulled up beside him, and he got into the car.

"Robyn!" he said (using my Christian name for the first time), "I have been forgiven!"

I had no idea what he was talking about, but, during the following week, I came to understand as Mr. Black revealed to me the story of his life. He had made and lost an immense fortune on two occasions. The first was from the illicit timber industry in Africa; the second was from running Asian opium dens. He had done every bad thing it was possible to do, with one exception: he had never killed anyone—although he had paid people to kill on his behalf. One incident that haunted him was seeing someone whom he had paid to be killed burn to death.

It was at his mother's funeral that he realized how wrong it was to live such a life. His mother had prayed for him all his life, and so too his sister, who was a missionary. At the funeral he came to believe that his mother had died from a broken heart because of his sinful life. He went to France and admitted himself into a monastery. He left after two years because he could not believe God could forgive him for what he had done. When he departed, the senior monk said to him that their monastery, and the sister monastery in England, would pray for him every day until they heard that he had come to believe God could forgive him. Eight years had gone by and, although he read the Scriptures diligently, he still had no understanding of God's forgiveness, until he spent that afternoon with my pastor.

Mr. Black and I worked together for just another ten days before he moved on to New Zealand. His manner changed completely, he became kind and friendly, even fatherly. During this time he was baptized by immersion. I will never forget his face as he came up from the water. He shone with joy as he revelled in the knowledge of sins washed completely away.

From New Zealand he wrote several times. One letter began, "The stars cannot tell, the moon cannot say, the change in me since Jesus came into my life." He went on to speak to many influential people around the world, telling them about Jesus.

I was the pastor in that story. Robyn has been a member of our church for decades. I had no idea of Mr. Black's background when he came to me, and he told me nothing about it. I simply explained to him how God forgives our sins through what Jesus did for us on the cross, asked him if he had made a commitment to God that embraced God's gift (he kind of replied he had), explained the issues about the baptism in the Holy Spirit, and prayed for him to receive that. His stiff British formality dominated the mood of our brief conversation, and the prayer time and result were unspectacular when I think of the hundreds I have prayed for like this. Except for one thing. When we finished praying, he lifted his head and stared at me, utter astonishment on every line of his face. Intrigued, I waited for him to explain, but slowly his expression changed and the British reserve returned. He politely thanked me and left. Only when Robyn got back to me later did I learn what God had done. Somehow the activity of the Holy Spirit enabled him to experience God in his life and revealed the favor of God in deleting his past. The speed and efficiency of God's work were remarkable.

God is good, and He supernaturally enters the lives of believers and changes them for the better, in all aspects of their lives. That's the premise of this book. If that is the case, the change in a new believer should also penetrate the wallet, as we will see in the next story.

Chapter 13
THE GIVER

Who Are the Most Generous?

CHRISTIANS SHOULD BE generous with their cash, willing to give to the poor and needy. That issue is measurable. It should be possible to get statistics that will demonstrate it to be true. Has anyone ever done that?

Who gives money to charities? Who are the Good Samaritans? What factors affect generosity?

US studies show that charity can be affected by several factors: the strength of the economy, tax policy, scandals among charities, and the kinds of appeals made. But one other beats them all—the character of the donor.

Research shows that a particular kind of person gives generously to charity. The same person also volunteers in the community. Ninety percent of volunteers contribute to charity, their households giving 2.6 percent of their income—considerably more than the national average.

Who are the big givers? One of the clearest research findings is that the volunteer/donor is likely to be an active Christian. So if you are looking for volunteers or givers forget income, age, race or education; just look for Christians. That's what numbers show.

Here are a few of those numbers:[1]

- In the US, about two-thirds (67 percent) of charitable giving comes from the 38 percent of Americans who go to church weekly.

- They give 3.4 percent of their weekly income. Those who attend church only a few times a year average just 1.4 percent, and those who don't attend average 1.1 percent.

- Do Christians confine their giving to their own churches and religious bodies? No. They do give to their own churches (which pass on a great deal to the community) but they give generously to other nonreligious organizations as well. Researcher Virginia Hodgkinson found that two-thirds of the money donated to *nonreligious* charities comes from church members.

- There is more. Christians separate into two broad groups— conservative (evangelical, Bible believing) and liberals. Conservative Christians gave more than the liberals, and the more conservative they were, the more they gave.

That study is a bit dated (1997), but a 2005 UK study, "How Christians use their money and why," published by Christian Research, reinforced the main points. It reported:

> On average, [evangelical Christians] give 7.5 percent of their income to churches and a further 3 percent to Christian charities. Kolaneci's research suggests they also give about 1.5 percent to secular charities.[2]

The overall average level of charitable giving in the UK (which would include giving by Christians) is estimated at 1.4 percent of after-tax household income.[3]

So once again, when there are needs, the wallets of Christians are easiest to open. Why is this? Most Christians are driven by faith in Jesus Christ, inspired by His story of the Good Samaritan (Luke 10:25–37) who rescued a beaten-up guy on the side of the road. Jesus said, "Go and do likewise" (v. 37). They are doing that. And it's a reflection of God at work in them. God is big and warm and generous, and those who walk with God inevitably pick up His characteristics.

It is time to direct our attention to God's enemy, the devil. Our culture fosters the belief that the devil is a myth. In fact he is very real, just as God is real. The Bible paints him as a roaring lion, prowling around the earth looking for someone to devour (1 Pet. 5:8). Multiple times Jesus cast out demons, freeing the oppressed from many appalling bondages. You can read about them in the Gospels. Does demonization still happen today? Or has modern science and education taken us "beyond" that? The next story lifts the lid on a world completely unknown to most.

Chapter 14
THE GAMING ADDICT

IN A BOOK about the reality and power of God, it shouldn't be surprising to find something on exorcism, the deliverance from demonic spirits. But a topic like that needs introduction, as few have knowledge of it, and the activities are sometimes incredible, even bizarre. The fact is, demonic spirits are real. Jesus confronts them at the beginning of His ministry, and quickly delegates the work of exorcism to His twelve disciples (Luke 9:1), then to seventy-two others (Luke 10:1–20). His last few words on earth include a specific commission to all believers for the task (Mark 16:17). Today, two thousand years later, believers are still casting out demons. All around the world, people continue to enjoy the benefits of authority over evil spirits. It is a little-known reality.

As mentioned above there are "bizarre" elements to demonization. Many biblical stories of demons are extraordinary. The Gerasenes demoniac of Mark 5 is a classic example. This poor man was possessed by thousands of demons (a "legion," or six thousand) so powerful they enabled him to break iron chains. He lived in the cemetery, terrorizing the neighborhood, crying out and cutting himself with stones. Jesus cast out all the spirits, which fled into about two thousand pigs that, in turn, rushed into a lake and drowned. The man was totally cured. That is bizarre! But the story (and many others related to exorcism) has a secure place in the New Testament, just as secure as the Sermon on the Mount, the Crucifixion story, the Resurrection story, and Jesus' command to love one another. We cannot embrace one part of Scripture and set aside another. So today we should expect to confront demonic activity and the need for casting out demons—in spite of our secular, unbelieving worldview. And we can expect bizarre elements with them.

The validity of exorcism ministry can be tested by its fruit. (See Matthew 7:15–20.) First, you look at the results of a deliverance process—are they good or bad? Is the person free from the problem, and happy? Second, is Jesus Christ the one giving mastery over the demons, and is He the one honored? In the following story you can judge for yourself. I can vouch for the storyteller because he is my son, Matthew Prince. So read this honest and remarkable depiction of how Jesus brought help from a modern-day problem.

In August 2011, on a whim, my friend Dan Faber invited an American minister friend of his, Pastor Jay Bartlett, to preach at his church in Dingley Village, Melbourne. Jay's ministry focus was deliverance—casting out demons. He was actually visiting Sydney, but he prayed about it and felt the real reason God had him in Australia was to visit Dingley Village in Melbourne.

Rachael (my wife) and I went along. I had a sneaking suspicion I needed deliverance from an evil spirit, and had asked Dan ahead of time if I could spend some time with Jay to get checked out. I bore a massive resentment to an old school friend (we will call him Max) who had hurt me very badly. I held bitterness, unforgiveness, anger and rage for many years and tried unsuccessfully many, many times to forgive and move on. I can't remember a single time when I hadn't felt anger, hatred, or discomfort when I saw him. But it was fifteen years since all that pain began and I thought things were relatively OK, as I didn't think about him too often anymore. Besides, he now lived overseas.

But that night, just before the meeting, Max walked in. It was a complete shock and just brought everything up again. I was civil and said hello, but was definitely standoffish and went home in a severely withdrawn state.

That night Rach forced the issue and I admitted being upset with all that old stuff thrown up in my face again. She understood but wasn't happy, and made a stand against it, firmly asserting our secure positions in Christ. That snapped me out of it, which was unusual, as typically I would withdraw and be resentful and angry until it passed. Nevertheless, at about 3:00 a.m. next morning I woke up, and for about an hour was plagued with hate-filled, murderous thoughts about Max until

I finally managed to get them out of my mind and went back to sleep.

On Wednesday morning, Jay and Dan came to my home. Jay began asking where I was at in my life, and family and personal history. My hate and unforgiveness for Max quickly reared its head, so Jay went to work. Using relevant scripture, we went through a repentance process. Jay was very clear about my need to forgive my brother, so I repented—genuinely repented.

Then, using the authority of the name of Jesus, communion, Bible verses, worship, and love, Jay prayed for me. Very quickly I felt "something" inside me. I knew what it was. Words and emotional reactions began to surface that I knew were not mine. Jay had instructed me that should I not restrict feelings or actions or emotions so that he could deal with the spirits. I assume this was so he would not be hampered by my defenses—by my being worried about what they would think of me. So I spoke the words and expressed the emotions. I could stop if I chose, but I was a part of them and fully immersed—I guess this would be called manifesting. My voice was different, my words and actions were not mine and I felt strong emotions like arrogance, extreme anger, hatred, mockery, fear, desperation, and more. Unusual physical sensations occurred—my arms had intense pins and needles, my throat became constricted and my tongue completely rigid at times. It was very strange, but I was not scared. Jay began asking questions of the spirits to get information that he needed. After a while he discovered five spirits: "No," Anger, Hatred, Filth, and Fear.

"No" was first. Its mission was to kill greatness: it was "No" to living, "No" to dreams, "No" to leadership, to keep me small and restricted. This was the strongest spirit at this point, and twice I struck the Bible out of Jay's hands as he read to me. The spirit became desperate, talking about his commission and how important it was for him to stay, but in the end he had to go. Jay commanded the other four spirits to join him. Their exit was quite uncomfortable, I felt an increasingly large "lump" in my throat that moved into my mouth and my tongue went rigid. But eventually, as Jay persisted with his commands and with physical effort on my behalf, I "coughed" the spirits out, declaring internally to myself at the same time that they were gone in that cough. Then I flopped back on the couch, my body relaxed—exhausted and at peace.

All up, Jay and Dan had prayed for three or four hours, but to me it felt like about thirty minutes.

A bit stunned by it all, I was not sure how to treat life from that point—I hadn't experienced deliverance before. I was subdued for a few days, but nevertheless excited and hopeful for the future. I immediately wanted to read the Bible, pray, pray in tongues, and spend time with God. This was very, very unusual for me.

Above all I noticed a complete change in attitude toward Max. All the hatred and unforgiveness was gone. Not a trace left. No resentment, no anger, no bitterness—nothing. For almost fifteen years I had tried to give it up and forgive him, with no success—now it was completely gone. Completely. I was utterly, utterly astounded and shocked.

After a couple of days praying and spending time with God, I noticed more "symptoms"—a lump in my throat and excessive negative reactions to the things of God. I became concerned and tried to ignore it, but it became obvious more stuff was there. Jay was leaving the next day and booked solid until his departure, so I offered to drive him to the airport to ask him about it. He was very encouraging and advised me to get more deliverance.

So I arranged for more prayer at the home of Dan's parents-in-law and invited Dan, Max, his wife (we will call her Angela), and my pastor Dan Parker to assist. Max was the most experienced in deliverance as he had worked with Jay for some time (and I note that Max is now a completely different man), but one of the first things he did was have me declare my submission to Pastor Dan, to establish his spiritual authority against the spirits. I look back with shame at my proud response as I hesitated, and agreed only with some reluctance.

So we began the evening, with a mixture of Bible verses, confession by me of stuff that was coming to mind, praying, communion, etc. After a while a spirit began manifesting. I experienced feelings of defiance, my eyes closed firmly, refusing communion, closing my mouth tight and on two occasions actually knocking the communion cup to the floor, spilling the contents; I felt a sense of horror at this. They were commanding the spirit to respond, to speak, to reveal its identity, but it refused and my experience was of smug, arrogant satisfaction. But as they persisted with the name of Jesus, the spirit began to snarl. It became obvious, and significant in view of what we had done at the start, that Pastor Dan had the most effect on the spirit—I believe because of his spiritual authority as my senior pastor.

The snarls became more aggressive—growls and occasionally roars—but the spirit still refused to speak. It escalated until, with my eyes still firmly closed, I stood slowly and walked to the middle of the room, growling and roaring, ignoring all commands from everyone. I was surprised that I could stand and walk, and experienced feelings of evil delight. I pointed my hands like a gun, arms outstretched, slowly moving it around the room—but was cut short by a command to put down the "weapon." Eventually, with a sense of utter evil satisfaction and ecstatic arrogance, the spirit spoke, "I am free."

After slowly moving my pointed arm around the room and not finding what I was looking for, I planted my feet squarely, lifted my arms, and roared, "come," again and again. Then I saw above me a large whirlwind of evil spirits. At that point my friend Dan, who is six foot seven inches tall, was thrown to the floor. He got up, was knocked down again, left the room quickly and fell down again. I opened my mouth, intending to draw the spirits into myself and unleash a mighty, unholy fury on the people around me. I thank God that at that moment Angela said, "TELL MATT TO COME BACK," and with that my full consciousness immediately returned. With utter horror I realized what I had been about to do, and I collapsed in hysterical tears, sobbing, "sorry, I'm so sorry" over and over while Angela hugged me.

After I had calmed down we discussed what had happened and the topic of gaming came up, and the fact that I was the leader of an online gaming clan (or club). As we were discussing whether I should give it up, the demon took over again and began shouting things like, "NO, THEY ARE MY MEMBERS," and "DON'T TOUCH THEM—I RECRUITED THEM." The others jolted me back—it was now very obvious what the spirit was connected to. Each time we tried to discuss it the spirit manifested more aggressively, until eventually Max said to the spirit, "Fine, it's fine—you can keep your members" in order to pacify it. I now felt I was going insane— as if the spirit and I were struggling for control. It was just beneath the surface and breaking through almost at will. I began to walk around the room with a glass of water saying, "water, drinking water" repeatedly so that I could focus on something and maintain control. Looking back, I am no longer critical of "crazy people" you see sometimes muttering to themselves in the street. I felt I was going insane, and was genuinely scared that I would not return to myself again.

After some time, I grew calmer and felt a little more in control. We had a problem though—when Dan left the room he had called the police because he was so concerned for our safety. Now four police cars sat out the front. The police wanted to talk with me to see if I was OK, but I didn't want to see them, so Pastor Dan made numerous trips back and forth to try to sort something out. They suggested ambulance officers checking me out, but it was going to be a long time before an ambulance was available. They kept insisting on seeing me, but I was extremely worried they would ask me what happened and cause the spirit to manifest. They carried guns and I knew I might not be able to control what happened. But eventually Pastor Dan convinced them to leave, and they did.

I was petrified of going home and having something trigger the manifestation near my wife and kids, so Pastor Dan arranged to spend the night with me and another pastor (Bryan) in a local hotel, for which I was so grateful. I felt the spirit stir several times during the night, but I was very conscious of the others there and it did not manifest again that night.

The next couple of days were not much fun, but Tuesday or Wednesday night we continued, this time with Pastor Dan, Pastor Tom (another church elder), and Pastor Bryan, meeting in Pastor Dan's office at the church. It was a hard slog. The spirit was heavily resistant, but at least communicating a bit more. I confessed relevant things I could think of when appropriate, and in the dialogue between Pastor Dan and the spirit, we discovered several other spirits. They were:

Sentinel (main spirit, whose job was to protect)

Mocking (pride)

Righteousness (we referred to this one as False Righteousness because when we asked for clarification it responded "Not YOUR righteousness—OUR righteousness")

Horde

Feasting

Lucifer (not the original— many spirits apparently take these names)

After much effort trying to cast out Sentinel, the pastors eventually decided fasting and praying were required, so we finished for the night.

The next day I made a conference call with Jay (and Max) to gain Jay's input. His feedback was:

Lots of encouragement, urging me to continue. He sees many people begin the process and then become fearful or deceived, so that they don't get rid of the spirits

The link between Sentinel and gaming was obvious and needed to be dealt with. Jay confirmed that my leadership of the gaming clan was a huge stronghold and when the spirit was summoning the whirlwind of spirits, he believed it was calling upon the spirits within the other members.

To break the power of that spirit, I had to destroy all physical connections and renounce my involvement and leadership of the clan.

Given the stubborn resistance from Sentinel, Max suggested going for the smaller spirits first, to weaken him and make him easier to deal with.

We met again that night with Pastor Dan, Pastor Bryan, and Kristin (my brother-in-law, who also had deliverance previously). I had brought Pastor Dan up to speed with Jay's feedback, so we began by creating a list of all my clan members. My job was to break any spiritual ties and repent. As we prayed, my feelings were of complete dismay and anger as Sentinel (and some of my own emotions) reacted. I had taken leadership of the clan about two years before, and poured my heart into building a stable, strong clan, recruiting members based on friendships and commitment. I had organized a number of events for members, who would sometimes travel from around Australia to hang out for several days at a time. I had spent thousands of hours building relationships with members and living in that environment. The clan was recognized and respected in Australia and around the world, the best in its field by a long way. So it was a big deal for me, but more so for Sentinel, who had hooked into other people also addicted to online gaming.

So we went through the list, one member at a time, breaking ties, renouncing, repenting. Some members provoked a violent reaction in Sentinel, shouting things like "No, not him!" and crying, but with the support of the guys and my own will, we worked through the entire list. The hardest part was renouncing my alias. All online gamers create an alias, which identifies them to other players. It's like your name, but only applies online. It essentially creates another identity, and because there is little accountability online the environment can be filthy and perverted. When I had to renounce my alias, it felt as though I was destroying a personality that was me. But I knew it was right, so in the name of Jesus I broke its hold and connections with me. Pastor Dan then charged me to never use that alias again, and destroy all connection to that false identity. I still felt the anguish of the severance, but readily agreed.

Sentinel was now weaker, but progress had stalled. I knew that for things to go ahead I had to destroy the physical connections with my old identity and sever ties with the clan, as Jay had said. So we finished for the night and set the next meeting for Friday. Kristin agreed to come back to my house with me as I destroyed my online entity and stuff to do with the clan. So I deleted all my online gaming accounts, and all accounts that used my alias identification. I completely deleted the clan website, made the clan domain name inaccessible, and deleted the gaming servers my clan owned and anything else related to gaming. I gave Kristin all my hard copies of games to throw out. Finally, that night I wrote a letter to all of the members in the clan, in the most sensitive way I could (without holding back), outlining exactly what had happened to me. I officially renounced my leadership, broke ties, renounced my old alias and declared I would now only be known by my real name. I finished by declaring that I would now be following Jesus.

That was one of the hardest e-mails I have ever written.

The next day, I went through and cleaned my external life from gaming. I gathered up my entire computer system, with monitors, a laptop, all computer equipment related to gaming, sound system, and anything else connected in some way, and took them to the tip and got rid of them—it was all high-end gaming equipment. I felt something of an idiot as people watched and asked what I was throwing out, but I threw it out anyway and quickly left.

I was impatient to get to the next deliverance session and relieved when the time came. Just prior to each deliverance, I felt incredibly nervous; a feeling that passed once we began. Others I spoke to reported feeling the same.

Pastor Dan, Pastor Bryan, and Kristin had already discussed strategy, which I later learned was to begin with weaker spirits and remove their rights (but not cast them out until the end). During the process I was fascinated to see the strong legal structure of the spiritual world. It seems there are a number of laws that spirits know and must operate within, and there is an order by which spirits recognize authority. The rights of the spirit seem to be foundational. A spirit cannot be compelled to leave a person if it has a right to stay there (e.g., if the person has some existing involvement in things like unforgiveness, sexual activity outside marriage, any other sins, negative feelings that have been harbored, a curse spoken by someone, a generational tie, and many, many more). Spirits gain entry by these rights and some seem to be able to accumulate more rights over time. The deliverance strategy is to destroy the power of the spirit by removing its rights—e.g., repent, forgive, break ties using the name of Jesus, return words spoken negatively as blessings, and much more. In these times I had to be completely open, which was humiliating and embarrassing at times, but absolutely necessary.

As Dan addressed the spirits, Sentinel responded. Dan bound it in the name of Jesus, told it to go back, and then dealt with the others one by one. Sentinel kept surfacing—his job was to protect the spirits—so on many occasions Dan had to send him down again while he dealt with the weaker ones.

Each spirit manifested differently, with different voices and even different postures and facial expressions. I was present and aware, allowing the manifestations to "flow through" me. At any point I could be addressed or called back. It was a strange experience, but I had no sense of embarrassment as they were manifesting.

The whole experience was very complex and is hard to lay out, but the major spirits and their reactions were as follows.

False Righteousness

In communicating with this spirit Dan discovered two sets of rights and it had also influenced two of my children. The rights were:

Generational rights (the spirit had been passed down from previous generations)

My wrong attitudes in the area of righteousness, appearance of righteousness, pride

So we stopped to deal with these. I broke all generational ties in the name of Jesus and then spent time confessing and repenting of my wrong attitudes and things I had done. That done, Dan commanded it to leave. It didn't initially, but we found a very specific right, which was dealt with and it had to go.

Lucifer

When Dan called up Lucifer, the response I experienced was fear and shock. It was actually a very small, weak spirit, totally dependent on the protection of Sentinel. When asked what rights it had, Lucifer said it had many small rights, but insisted they were small and not worth worrying about. Dan asked how many rights it had and it immediately responded: fifty-seven. So Dan commanded it to list them all. With some "encouragement" Lucifer began. Kristin wrote them down, but didn't keep count. There were things like not giving when I was meant to, false patience, manipulating, independence, and so on.

Eventually, when Dan ordered the spirit to identify the next right it just stopped, and when we counted there were exactly fifty-seven. The extraordinary thing was that nobody had kept count, and I certainly had no sense of how many it had named.

At that point, it was pretty clear what to do. In front of the others I confessed and repented of every single sin on that list, one by one, not holding anything back. When it was all done, Dan called back Lucifer and asked if there were any more rights. The answer was "no," and he cast it out.

Horde

Pastor Dan called up Horde and the immediate response was, "Who are you and what is your authority?" Dan told Horde he was my senior pastor and I had submitted to his leadership and authority. I sensed that Horde was satisfied with that response and acknowledged that authority.

Horde was actually an army of spirits, whose leader, "No," had been cast out the week before by Jay. Horde was incredibly unemotional, communicating like a soldier awaiting orders—not caring what they were, just willing to follow orders that came through the correct lines of authority. At one point Kristin addressed the spirit, and it asked who he was and what his authority was. Horde refused to talk with him—I sensed because it would only communicate with the "highest ranked" authority.

Without a leader, Horde was useless, inactive, and actually asked to leave. It was essentially a dormant army waiting for orders that would never come. So Dan ordered it out, and with very little effort, it was gone.

Mocking (Pride)

For a long time Mocking gave only mocking smiles and sniggers. Eventually it spoke, and would have talked much if Dan had allowed it. It was essentially a spirit of pride, but was mocking. Its rights were the sin of pride, rejoicing in the weakness of others, addiction to pride, and the sin of mocking. The initial right was created when it entered through family lines—generational through the grandfather—and it had passed through to all three of my children.

Mocking delighted in passing spirits through generations, describing it as "beautiful" and as simple as a river flowing downhill. It was dismayed and confused as to why we would want to stop that. But, stop it we did. In the name of Jesus I broke all generational ties, then spent time commanding the spirit to leave my children. I broke the addiction in the name of Jesus and confessed and repented of the sins it had listed, not holding anything back. I was mad it had done so much in my life and intended the same for my kids. I recognized pride as a core sin in my life and *absolutely* wanted it out by the power and name of Jesus.

Feasting

Feasting was a fat, bloated, gluttonous spirit that we discovered was the source of addiction in my life. It didn't care what the addiction was, it would feast on it. It used words such as "tasty," "good meal," and so on, when describing sins and addictions. The addictions it listed (past and present) were gaming, pride (its main food), new things, prayer, reading the Bible, pornography, power and pride, food and alcohol.

One right was hidden and Feasting was scared to talk about it. After much probing the spirit weakened, and told us this right was held by another spirit—Domination. It begged us not to tell Domination who had revealed him.

So we noted that, then I confessed, repented, and broke powers, holding nothing back. In spite of that, Feasting still wouldn't go—we had to break the last right (Domination). So Dan called up this spirit.

Domination

Domination was very, very angry and aggressive—furious because he had been found out, and demanding to know who dobbed him in. Dan basically ignored that and ordered it to list its rights. After some pushing the spirit said there were instances of dominating and being dominated through my life. It didn't care whether it was dominating or being dominated—as long as domination was happening.

The initial right was given just after birth. At that point I had a clear picture in my mind of me as a newborn baby on a small table, surrounded by doctors and nurses in full gowns, face masks, and caps. Domination said it came through a doctor then. I was completely vulnerable and the doctor had a wrong spirit. My parents confirmed the incident. They remembered a particularly officious pediatrician present at my birth who abruptly whisked me away to be examined. His manner was so odd it stuck in their minds.

The spirit also said it had shown itself to my children, creating fear. "Fear is my child," it said. So again, I went through everything—breaking, confessing, and repenting.

Dan then cast out Domination and called up Feasting. Feasting was very upset that Domination had gone, calling him "my husband." Dan and the others got to work, commanding it to leave in the name of Jesus. At that moment I felt a large lump in my stomach—I actually physically felt it and was really worried because I hadn't experienced this lump before—the size of a large orange. I somehow knew what to do, though, and used my hands to push it up slowly. I could actually feel it rising through my chest, to my neck, then through my throat and mouth, and then finally I "flung" it out of my body and it was gone. I had never before experienced anything like that.

Sentinel

Sentinel had several times interrupted our dealings with other spirits, but was now desperate because the spirits it was protecting had gone. After some prodding it revealed its mission. It belonged to an Order (I sensed something like an Order of Knights, where duty and mission are core values) and had passed through male blood and was generational. Its job was to guard—nothing specific—but an encompassing role to prevent Godliness entering and to protect things of the devil. It was also guarding my heart.

At that point I had another clear picture—of a door with a significant keyhole. I knew it was the door to my heart that Sentinel was guarding. I told Dan, so he pushed in again and Sentinel eventually revealed that the One who held the key was the Holy Spirit.

We stopped again and broke the power of the spirit, then returned and, with much commanding, Sentinel was compelled to leave and he was gone.

We were so happy. Dan, Bryan, and Kristin were ecstatic and cheering. I was happy, but exhausted. So we finished up and I walked out to the car by myself.

Before driving off, I sat in the car and thought about the door and the key. I said, "Holy Spirit, please use the key You have." A clear picture formed in my mind and I watched a swirling wind of light place the key in the lock and open the door. Light poured through the door and the surrounding walls began to crack, before collapsing completely and disappearing. What was left was my heart—perfect and white and glowing and shining. In awe I reached for it and held it in my hands. Lifting it above my head, I said, "Here Jesus, this is Yours." Jesus reached down and took my heart in His hands with the greatest love. Then slowly He descended into me so that my body was completely encompassed by His, and, still holding my heart in His hands, He stopped when my heart was back in its place in my body—now held by Jesus. My feeling at that point can only be described as intense happiness and peace. I still have this feeling whenever I remember this experience.

Over the next few days I felt tired and somewhat dead, a bit unsure of what happened. Sometimes I thought the spirits were back, as I could feel lumps in my throat or old feelings recurred. But they were all lies, absolute lies. I learned that spirits try to return to rob the person of their freedom, but all that is required is to tell them to leave in the name of Jesus. So when I experienced old feelings I told them to go in Jesus' name, and every time they did and I felt free again. Sometimes I had to war for an hour, but mostly a one- or two-minute prayer has been enough. When I do experience the old feelings I am taken by surprise. They no longer feel natural. I praise our Almighty God for what He has done in me.

Here are some of the "befores" and "afters." Some—certainly not all. These are the changes I noticed immediately and during the following couple of weeks.

Patience with kids

Before: Often easily frustrated with the children, especially in times of stress. I would regularly go to my study and leave my wife with them. I would often get angry and treat them harshly and my anger would pervade the house and ruin family evenings.

After: I am almost never frustrated to the point of anger by my children. I am much more patient and so much more loving and understanding. I am firm, but do not get angry. Evenings are rarely unpleasant, and never because of my anger.

Relationship with my wife

Before: I didn't want to spend time with Rach, as I wanted to do my own thing, especially getting on the computer, gaming, or watching TV shows. If I spent time with her it was because that was a good thing that a husband should do, and I did want her to be happy. However, my focus was always on "completing the task" so I could go and do my own thing. I would go to bed much later than her in order to spend time on the computer. Then I would get up much later in the morning. I would often express anger and scorn, and look down on her, and give disapproving and negative looks. It would be extremely rare for me to share myself honestly with her. She tried many times to bring God into our relationship more, but I was largely disinterested and tried to avoid it.

After: I love spending time with Rach—she is my precious jewel and I will never forget what she went through because of me in her commitment and love for me. She has forgiven me and is so much happier. I love being with her, talking, praying together, even just being in the same room together. I always try to go to bed at the same time as her, as I don't want to be disconnected, and I rise very soon after her in the morning. I have confessed and repented of many things that have hurt her over the years. I am now the spiritual head of the house. I pray for the kids and for her. I bind the enemy's influence, and am leading our kids in loving Jesus. My stepping into this role has made a profound difference to our family.

Gaming

Before: I had periods where I would game sixty to eighty hours per week. My normal pattern was to game four to five hours in the evenings and two to three hours during the day.

After: Jesus has completely broken my addiction. My desire for gaming has gone. There have been two or three occasions since when I have felt drawn back, but I rebuked those attacks in the name of Jesus and they stopped.

Relationship with Jesus

Before: I was resigned to where I was. I had tried stuff, prayed for change, but nothing significant had happened. I had received encouraging words from God, but felt guilty about them and resigned to inaction. I read my Bible little and prayed only occasionally, attending church weekly.

After: I want to spend all my time with Jesus. I have been so astounded by His grace, and grateful for it. I didn't deserve or ask for this change, but He came in and completely turned my life around, dealing with lifelong issues within a matter of hours. I am now spending time with God like never before—it is the thing that has replaced gaming. I love hearing His voice, reading His Word, and praying. I had never really understood loving Jesus, but I now know.

Fatherhood of my kids

Before: I would be happy to play with them, but often joked around in a way that was confusing to them. I would sometimes be encouraging, but very quick to come down on them.

After: I am building God into their lives with prayer and by speaking God into them. I have confessed and repented appropriately before them and asked their forgiveness for my behavior. I express far more love and understanding to them. In return they have become much, much more responsive and loving toward me, with cuddles, kisses, writing cards, drawings and just talking.

Unforgiveness

Before: I had tried my best to deal with my unforgiveness for Max without success. Though I thought it had faded out enough to not be an issue anymore, I did not want to see him ever again and would not have let him near my family.

After: He is completely forgiven by me. I look forward to catching up next time, and I have no ill feelings toward him. It wouldn't upset me if he came and lived on my street.

Pride

Before: It would take pages to cover all this. My life has been saturated with pride. I have been distant from people because of it, and it influenced every single part of my life. After: I am still dealing with this—as you might deal with a lifelong habit. The power and hold of it is broken, but now I am working with the ingrained thinking patterns. I am learning how much God has done for me and how I don't deserve it at all, which highlights further just how much He loves me.

I was nothing.

But You loved me.

You are God.

Everything is Yours.

Getting into Gaming

I grew up with gaming. Our first computer, a Commodore 64, loaded games via a cassette player. Like other kids, I loved playing, especially with friends. Starting with platform shooters, arcade games, puzzles etc, I progressed to simulators, first-person shooters (FPS) and role-playing games (RPG).

I developed a love for FPS, running around and killing your gaming opponents. I became proficient, refining head shots (instant kills), adjusting aim for ping (aiming ahead of target to compensate for online delays), learning spawn points (knowing where and when special weapons, powerups and vehicles would appear), knowing enemy location, making myself a hard target (strafing, jumping, and using obstacles), knowing grenade points (to bounce and create unexpected effects), becoming extremely proficient with vehicles, and much, much more.

Team games were my favorite as they provided a live environment of cooperation and teamwork. Adrenaline and glory are the rewards—action is fast and nonstop, with limitless potential outcomes to ever-varied situations.

To be a solid performer takes hundreds of hours, but to become really good takes thousands (one thousand hours is like six months of full-time work). Over the years I played some games for thousands of hours, some for hundreds.

Nobody uses their real name in gaming—everyone creates an alias. It becomes a part of you, but is separate. I bonded to my name, but also used it as an excuse to be someone else. With no restrictions or accountability, this was easy to do, and I would often pour out horrible abuse and foul language on players without regard for their feelings or age. This was not immediate; initially I was shocked by language and attitudes. But eventually I became immune, and as my conscience was seared, I behaved the same way.

I got to know some people who were part of the same clan, a kind of exclusive club, with special privileges and rights. I joined, and eventually became leader. It was the most established and respected clan in our gaming community, with the most restrictive membership requirements. Like a family, every night, and often during the day, between two and twenty of us gathered online. We talked through headsets, gaming together, talking teamwork and just having fun.

My gaming increased and I began to resent intrusions on my gaming time, even activities with family and friends. My wife felt undervalued, unloved and alone, not knowing what to do. She raised the issue several times, but I resisted. Sometimes we agreed on restrictions, but they inevitably gave way to the magnetism of gaming. I was addicted.

My problem was not unique. Complaints about "interfering" girlfriends and wives are common in the gaming community. I fear today's gamers will leave a generation of "virtual widows" and fatherless children.

I finally began a Role-Playing Game (RPG), which required even longer stretches of time, as teammates were highly dependent on each other. This put even more stress on my marriage and family life. Once my six-year-old daughter asked me to do something with her. I said no, because I was gaming and my teammates were depending on me. She replied, "Daddy, you should love your kids more than the game." My heart was so hard that I laughed and justified myself, then told her to leave. I was completely absorbed with myself, acknowledging God and going to church, but blind to the fact that I was addicted and it was ruining my relationships with my wife and family and God.

In my deliverance process it became absolutely clear that Satan was using my gaming addiction and ties with other addicted gamers to keep me bound up and away from the presence of God. I was shocked to my core to discover the impact these spirits had in my life, all the while hidden from my sight.

Afterward I realized that Satan had done a deal with me without my explicit consent. Satan gave me a false life filled with immediate gratification: adrenaline, excitement, and respect. In return, he took my real life; and that's exactly what gaming is when it becomes an addiction—a means of stealing real life. When there is no alternative to living life passionately, it becomes a logical, easy option.

Now I occasionally game, but it is with my daughters, playing Mario Kart on the Wii with them, where I am building relationship rather than destroying it. It is only by His grace that I was saved from those evil spirits, and I lift up the name of Jesus, the name above all names, the name that saved me from gaming.

Following that process Matthew gathered a few friends and they prayed together regularly and also went out praying for many others for healing and deliverance. They have seen many remarkable miracles. And he joined a group who travelled to Mexico for a short trip to pray for sick and demonized there. Here are some extracts from his report:

Mexico

August 2012

Well, it's time to update—so much has happened.
Worship times are amazing. God's presence is so powerful,
and worship can easily go for two to three hours.
The power of God has just kicked in. Here are my personal
testimonies so far:

Twelve-year-old girl couldn't see properly out of left eye.
Prayed a couple of times, then she could see perfectly (covered right eye and got her to read stuff). She was so happy
she was crying. Prophesied over her that her destiny was not
obvious, hidden, but she wasn't to worry because one day
God would just pick the shell up off the beach and blow in
it and the purpose of the shell would be known. It obviously
impacted her—there was peace and joy on her face. My interpreter (Ruby) was so touched she was having trouble inter-
preting because she was crying with joy. I cried a bit, too.

Seventeen-year-old boy had swelling in left chest area which
doctors could not identify or fix. It has prevented him from
playing sports. He was healed and could breathe deeply—first
time since he has had the swelling. He was crying he was so
relieved and happy.

Five-year-old girl healed of a sore tummy. So cute—she
gave me a hug afterward, which was better than seeing her
healed (for me).

Man had pain in thighs and groin—pain level went from
a 10 to a 3.

Man had prostate cancer and bad knees. Knees healed and
feeling of holy peace. Unable to tell if prostate cancer was healed.

Woman in wheelchair had arthritis and severe pain in
back. Pain in back completely gone; pain in knees gone. Tried
to walk three times—each time was much more successful
than the last (the first time was painful because of back,
second time was painful because of knees, and third time it
was just tiring!). Felt strong heat throughout her body—her
hands were very hot to touch.

Next day

The twelve-year-old girl who couldn't see properly out of her left eye came for prayer. Her eye was still completely healed—she was just afraid it would go bad again.

A five-year-old girl healed of a sore throat.

Prayed for a man on dialysis—kidneys. He said he felt heat and peace (healing not able to be confirmed as there was no pain anyway).

Prayed for a man to be delivered of a spirit of anger—he felt deep peace afterward. He also had pain in the back of his neck that had been with him for a while (7/10 rating) which disappeared completely after praying.

An older man with a bad knee (pain 6/10) and couldn't walk properly came and this time I got my interpreter (Ruby) to pray for him. She was nervous, but stepped up and prayed like I had been praying. The pain went from 6 to 3, then from 3 to 1, then from 1 to 0. At the end he was squatting up and down with no pain. Ruby was stoked.

A different man began to manifest a spirit of anger up the front while receiving prayer. He was on the ground yelling and struggling. Lots of people jumped in, but I told them to leave, then took him aside with Shane (interpreter) and prayed. He manifested a bit more, but I found out the demons were there because of hate for family. He broke down and cried and I hugged him, then I prophesied that he would be a giver of love to people—a safe, gentle person. He then repented of the hate and I got rid of the spirit. It went immediately, and he felt complete peace. He was so happy, he introduced his wife and baby daughter to me and I prayed a blessing over the little girl, then he got photos with me holding his daughter with him and his wife.

There were many, many more stories like these from Matthew. Space limits us to these few. So there is fruit of the ministry of deliverance that God, in His grace, has given to His people.

Chapter 15
THE DESPERATE COUPLE

J ESUS GAVE ALL His followers authority over evil spirits. His achievements through the Cross and Resurrection—the defeat of sin, death, and the devil—were all passed on to believers, though many are unaware of it. That is the basis and authority for casting out demons. But it raises an interesting question: can nonbelievers cast out demons? What happens if they try? Here is one example.

This story came from Pastor Arthur Westbrook from Mossman in Far North Queensland, Australia. He has five sisters and one brother and all have been active in Christian ministry. Several of the family have served as missionaries in Papua New Guinea, notching up a total of 130 years of missionary service in that country. We were swapping miracle stories and he told me this one. Before reading it, have a look at this passage from the Book of Acts. The similarity is obvious:

> Some Jews who went around driving out evil spirits tried to invoke the name of the Lord Jesus over those who were demon-possessed. They would say, "In the name of the Jesus whom Paul preaches, I command you to come out." Seven sons of Sceva, a Jewish chief priest, were doing this. One day the evil spirit answered them, "Jesus I know, and Paul I know about, but who are you?" Then the man who had the evil spirit jumped on them and overpowered them all. He gave them such a beating that they ran out of the house naked and bleeding.
>
> —ACTS 19:13–16

From Pastor Arthur Westbrook

One afternoon there was a knock on my front door. I opened it to find a man standing there, dripping wet. He told me he was in trouble and that someone had told him I could help.

Standing behind him was his wife—also dripping wet. The story they told and what happened next I will never forget.

There had been a massive building boom in the Douglas Shire in Far North Queensland. Huge tourist resorts were built in many places, changing the sleepy region from a rural sugar and fishing district to a world-renowned tourist destination. People today flock to the area to visit the Great Barrier Reef and the tropical rain forests.

One of the construction companies had brought a construction foreman to the region with his wife to work on one of the new developments. The man had a very important and responsible position, but his wife was at a loose end at home and became interested in the occult. As she became more deeply involved, she found herself writing on paper different scripts in many languages, then having her writings translated into English. It was all demonically inspired, but she was not aware of the dangers. She hoped to make money by selling the writings. But the activities eventually led to the demonization of her mind. Her behavior became erratic, and her husband, alarmed by what he was seeing, went home for lunch each day to check on her well-being. They couple had no church background and very little biblical understanding.

One day the husband came home to find his wife extremely agitated. Desperate for a solution, he apparently sensed that the problem had some sort of spiritual basis, so he decided to tackle it with the only religious act he could think of, which was baptism. So he took her to a popular picnic spot at a sandbar on the local river, where I have baptized many people myself. On arrival, the two of them walked out into the deeper water where the wife could be immersed in a ritual baptism.

As the husband began to lower her under the water, the spirit controlling his wife began to manifest, giving her incredible strength. Under the influence of the spirit, she grabbed her husband and threw him down, holding him under the water. The man almost drowned before he was able to escape her grasp. It was a serious near calamity. Eventually he managed to put his wife in the car and brought her up the street to the first church he could find to seek help. No one was there, so he went to another. There he found the minister and explained his problem, but this man had no experience in evicting demons. However, he directed him to a little shop on the corner; the people there went to a local Assemblies of God church—maybe they could help. The couple there directed them to my home, not far away.

So there they were—a wet, bewildered man, and a bedraggled, wet, troubled woman standing behind him. Very quickly he told me his story. I invited them in to sit down in our little front room where I often counseled people. The husband sat in one corner, the wife sat opposite. As I looked at her I could see her eyes were a picture of torment.

I explained that I had no power myself but I did have at my disposal all heaven's authority and power—more than enough to bring release from the evil spirits that were disturbing her. Jesus, I told her, had been sent to Earth to destroy the works of the devil, and through the power of the Holy Spirit and the blood of Jesus she would be set free. Then I pointed my finger at her and, looking straight into her eyes, commanded the tormenting spirit to come out of her and go.

There was a violent manifestation in the woman's body that lifted her off the floor to the ceiling. It was quite extraordinary. As I kept commanding the spirit to come out, she fell down, passing through the doorway into the kitchen and coming to rest partly under the kitchen table, where she lay like a dead corpse. I told the husband his wife was fine and would be completely normal when she got up. This lady had met the Master, Jesus Christ, and was completely delivered by the power of God.

I saw them only once after that. I happened to be driving through their hometown, a couple of hours south, when I pulled up at a set of traffic lights. To my surprise, they pulled up right beside me. It was one of those God events. I was able to ask how they were doing and they happily told me everything was fine.

If only people would turn to Jesus in the first place and discover the joy of salvation!

Jesus is there for desperate people.

Deliverance from demonic power is a fascinating subject. When people relate their stories, everyone listens! Another captivating subject open to the miracle-working power of God is sex. What does God say about that? Well God has much to say about sex. It is woven right through the Bible.

How is it treated? Is it a list of impossible kill-joy rules that no one can keep, or something that really works? Here is a short summary. You be the judge. After that we will see how God worked His power in the life of one man and his wife-to-be.

Chapter 16
GOD AND SEX
The Maker's Handbook

I N A WORLD gone mad on sex, we should ask, "What does God have to say about it?" In fact, He has much to say about sex because He made us, and sex was part of the package. Sex was God's idea. So, we do well to follow the Maker's instructions. Probably no other aspect of life can engender such happiness, fulfillment, and blessing if we follow God's directions. On the other hand, so much heartache, frustration, and pain follow if we ignore those directions.

Look what God says—start with some key verses:[1]

> So God created man in his own image...male and female he created them. God blessed them and said to them, "Be fruitful and increase in number."
> —GENESIS 1:27–28, NIV1984

We were created by God, in His image. Our capacity for sex and reproduction was part of creation. The command to multiply is fundamental to God's plan, and involves sex.

> For this reason a man will leave his father and mother and be united to his wife, and they will become one flesh.
> —GENESIS 2:24–25, NIV1984

"One flesh" is the heart of this passage. It refers to the sexual union of a man and woman. Jesus used these verses as the basis for marriage in Matthew 19:4–5.

However, God set boundaries to sex. Look at this:

> The lips of an adulteress drip honey, and her speech is smoother than oil; but in the end she is bitter as gall...Her feet go down to death; her steps lead straight to the grave.
> —PROVERBS 5:3–5, NIV1984

A strong warning to men, but followed by a beautiful portrayal of God's plan:

> Drink water from your own cistern, running water from your own well....May your fountain be blessed, and may you rejoice in the wife of your youth. A loving doe, a graceful deer—may her breasts satisfy you always, may you ever be captivated by her love.
>
> —PROVERBS 5:15, 18–19, NIV1984

Clearly it is "wife only," and, in that case, the Bible describes sex in glowing, positive terms and as a uniting, pleasurable experience.

First Corinthians 7:2–5 is the most comprehensive New Testament passage on sex and marriage (NIV1984):

> But since there is so much immorality, each man should have his own wife, and each woman her own husband. The husband should fulfill his marital duty to his wife, and likewise the wife to her husband. The wife's body does not belong to her alone but also to her husband. In the same way, the husband's body does not belong to him alone but also to his wife. Do not deprive each other except by mutual consent and for a time, so that you may devote yourselves to prayer. Then come together again so that Satan will not tempt you because of your lack of self-control.

SEX BEFORE MARRIAGE (FORNICATION) AND SEX OUTSIDE MARRIAGE (ADULTERY)

The Bible says, "Marriage should be honored by all, and the marriage bed kept pure, for God will judge the adulterer and all the sexually immoral" (Heb. 13:4).

God clearly placed sex inside the security and holiness of marriage, the lifelong commitment between a man and a woman. Anything outside this is against His will—for good reason. Enduring stability in marriage flows from a commitment enshrined in solemn vows, each partner promising to love the other "for better for worse... till death do us part." Given the variability and unreliability of romantic love, love of this other kind is the strongest guarantee for security and longevity in marriage. It is called sacrificial love, a love that gives simply for the sake of giving. Sacrificial love inspires love in the other partner, so love is continually renewed. So marriage, by means of the formal commitment—the vows and the blessing of God—is a hedge of protection.

Figures bear this out. Statistics show that people who are married have more stable relationships. Britain's Office for National Statistics studied 750,000 couples who completed a census in 1991 and 2001. Of the married couples, 82 percent were still living together in 2001; but of unmarried couples living together, only 61 percent were still together.[2]

Stresses and differences in Christian marriage are worked out through the love and commitment each promised—to serve the other. The secular model is the reverse; it says: "I will try living with you. If you satisfy my needs, I will stay. If you don't, I will leave and look for another who does." This selfish philosophy is doomed to failure.

Many passages warn against sexual immorality. Read: Romans 13:13; 1 Corinthians 6:13, 18-20; 10:8; Galatians 5:19; Ephesians 5:3; Colossians 3:5 and 1 Thessalonians 4:3–8.

HOMOSEXUALITY

That God intended sex to be confined to a man and a woman is clear, even from a basic study of anatomy. Remembering that God designed and created our bodies, it is plain that man was designed for woman and woman for man. (See 1 Corinthians 6:9.) And the Bible speaks clearly:

> The wrath of God is being revealed from heaven against all the godlessness and wickedness of men...Even their women exchanged natural relations for unnatural ones. In the same way the men also abandoned natural relations with women and were inflamed with lust for one another. Men committed indecent acts with other men, and received in themselves the due penalty for their perversion.
>
> —ROMANS 1:18, 26–27, NIV1984

God did not create people as homosexuals, just as He did not create people as adulterers. The idea that God would create a person designed to disobey Him is abhorrent. However, it is plain that some people suffer temptations toward homosexuality, just as others are tempted toward adultery or fornication. Such temptations are not from God and we are all required to resist them and seek help when we struggle. It is the task of the church to recognize the anguish suffered by such people and help them overcome. Compassion, mercy, and forgiveness are essential.

PORNOGRAPHY

Jesus spoke directly about the temptation faced by men in pornography:

> Anyone who looks at a woman lustfully has already committed adultery with her in his heart. If your right eye causes you to sin, gouge it out and throw it away. It is better for you to lose one part of your body than for your whole body to be thrown into hell.
>
> —MATTHEW 5:28–29, NIV1984

He was not speaking of literal eye gouging; He was simply highlighting a sober truth—men are tempted through the eye, and it is a serious problem. Men and women are different—men are visually attracted to women, while women are attracted to men by kind words and warm attention. Both men and women must guard their reactions. For men pornography is a unique and grave problem, and its impact is far more than emotional. The male brain is wired in such a way that addictive chemicals are released when viewing porn, the same chemicals that contribute to the grip of drug addiction. This explains pornography's terrible addictive power.

This is serious enough, but even worse is pornography's violation: of the wife, of the covenant relationship, of God's holy plan for the man's life, and of the women—real people—who create and are exploited by porn. These are the hideous evils of pornography. It is a sick, satanic blight on God's noble creation.

Divorce

Key scriptures are:

> So they are no longer two, but one. Therefore what God has
> joined together, let man not separate.
>
> —Matthew 19:6, niv1984
>
> Has not the Lord made them one? In flesh and spirit they are
> his. And why one? Because he was seeking godly offspring.
> So guard yourself in your spirit, and do not break faith with
> the wife of your youth. "I hate divorce," says the Lord God
> of Israel.
>
> —Malachi 2:15–16, niv1984

God's clear intent is that marriage is for life. However, in Matthew
19 Jesus refers to God's begrudging (Old Testament) permission for
divorce, acknowledging men's hardness of heart. In 1 Corinthians
7, Paul reinforces lifetime commitment in marriage, but allows a
person to remarry if the spouse has left him/her (v. 15). Note that
the word *bound* in verse 15 and the word *unmarried* in verse 27
come from the same Greek word, normally translated divorce. So
verses 27–28 become, "Are you married? Do not seek a divorce. Are
you unmarried [divorced]? Do not look for a wife. But if you do
marry you have not sinned."

The bottom line is that God planned marriage for life, and couples experiencing stress in marriage can be confident of willing
help from God.

Singles

Paul was single and celibate, and he held this up as an ideal way
to live—for those who are able to do so. He discusses this in 1
Corinthians 7.

Summarizing

So the Bible deals clearly with the major issues relating to sex. Its
teaching opens the door to every good thing God intended in this
significant part of life on Earth. The alternative may be alluring, but

disaster lurks at the door. The astute follow God's high plan and find happiness and fulfillment. It's a no-brainer.

Marriage Perks

Research shows that, on average, married people:[3]
Live longer
Earn more
Have greater wealth
Enjoy greater sexual satisfaction more often
Are less likely to suffer from mental health problems
Have less frequent breakups than unmarried couples who live together
Are less likely to break up when they don't live together before marriage
Have kids who are happier
Have kids who do better at school

MORE MARRIAGE PERKS

Another study (The New Family Structures Study—NFSS) by Dr. Mark Regnerus has also lifted the lid on perks enjoyed by the married. A survey of a random sample of about three thousand American young adults (ages eighteen to thirty-nine) provided fascinating information on how differing family arrangements affected the development of children. It compared social, emotional, and relational issues of young adults raised by a single parent, stepfamily, divorced, adopted family, or a gay father or lesbian mother, to those raised by married biological parents.[4]

The survey analyzed forty issues such as employment, welfare dependence, whether or not they voted, were they bullied, suicidal tendencies, problems requiring therapy, affairs, STIs, rape, education, health, happiness, depression, quality of relationships, use of marijuana/alcohol/cigarettes/TV, trouble with the law, number of sex partners, parents' education/income, and so on.

The survey was important for two reasons. First, understanding these issues is essential for the well-being and development of children. Second, some studies had claimed that children from alternative family structures (e.g., divorced, single parent, step-parent, etc.) were no worse off than children from two-parent married families—contrary to long-held views. However, concerns had been raised about the quality of research that had produced these findings. It was hoped that the NFSS, with careful planning and a large, random sample size, would produce a more reliable result. Other sociologists were consulted before and after the NFSS study and essentially endorsed the basic methodology and findings—despite protests from some interest groups impacted by the results.

The results were clear and unambiguous. With very few exceptions, the biological children of parents who were still married did best on every indicator. They were less dependent on welfare, more likely to be employed, more likely to vote, less likely to contemplate suicide, less likely to receive therapy, less likely to have affairs while in a relationship, less likely to have STIs, less likely to have been sexually touched by an adult, less likely to have been forced to have sex, better educated, closer to parents, healthier, happier, suffered less depression, enjoyed higher income, were less likely to have trouble in a relationship, and so on.[5]

For many of the indicators the differences were considerable. For example, the study looked at what percentage of each group was currently on public assistance. For children of still married biological parents, 10 percent were currently on public assistance, compared with 30 percent of those raised by a single parent; stepfamily, 30 percent; divorced parents, 32 percent; adopted, 41 percent; gay father, 34 percent; and lesbian mother, 26 percent.[6]

On the issue of ever being forced to have sex against your will, 8 percent of children of biological still-married parents responded yes, compared with 16 percent of those raised by a single parent; stepfamily, 16 percent; divorced parents, 24 percent; adopted, 23 percent; gay father, 25 percent; and lesbian mother, 31 percent.[7]

What is the reason behind the differences?

Dr. Regnerus went to great pains to say that the survey did not reveal causality; in other words, it is not possible to conclude that any of these family structures was the cause of poor results. Other studies are needed to determine that, he advised. And while the figures revealed distinct trends, there were many *individual* cases where children of alternative family structures did have good results. Nevertheless, it gave the overwhelming conclusion that children of the biological, still-married parents are likely to be far better off than children from all alternative family structures.

Really, that result should not be surprising. God created men and women and provided each with unique, different qualities designed to provide children with all they need in their development, in an environment of loving commitment as promised in the marriage vows. When either father or mother is absent in child raising and their unique gifts lost, and the marriage commitment is not honored, the child is inevitably disadvantaged.

That doesn't prove the existence of God, of course. But it is another factor that strongly bears out what we see in creation and read in the Bible. For believers these things are self-evident and don't need the confirmation of extensive surveys. It is simple: believe and enjoy.

Experiencing God Is Like…Hmmm

This is a little out of left field, but it ties in with the God and sex theme.

Finding God is like discovering buried treasure, a rare and rich thing. There is a downer trying to explain what you found. Preconceptions and objections can bring to a grinding halt even the most brilliant mind when you try to describe your relationship with your new friend Jesus. Visions of spoil-sport rules, do-good philosophies, boring lifestyles, perceived inconsistencies in the lives of believers, and pie in the sky when you die all rear their heads. When I became a Christian, that's how I saw it. Instead I was wonderfully surprised by what I found. But when I tried to explain it to others, their reaction was just like mine had been.

Finding and knowing God is not the only matter that challenges description. Many life topics are the same, and can only be truly understood by diving in and finding out first-hand. At the risk of being misunderstood, I suggest the subject of sex is a classic example. You notice it when you explain sex to children for the first time. A friend of mine was trying to explain things for his son, but when he came to the part that matters, he received a shocked "Aw, yuk!" in response. The boy was appalled. I have no doubt he softened that view eventually. All his objections, as great as they were on that day, ultimately would have crumbled in the face of experiences that were impossible for his dad to verbalize.

Sex is God's gift, very special and unique. In a much, much greater way, so is God's gift of Himself to us. Just as you use words to describe sex, so you can use words to describe a relationship and experience with God, but none do it justice. They are just a poor shadow of the reality.

The child who can't grasp the idea of sex has to be content with some basic information to ease the fears. First is the assurance of the parent or a trusted person in the world of a child. Second is the new understanding of the quirky aspects of our bodies, and the explanation for the stark reality of babies born every day (and it wasn't the stork). Then there is the witness of millions of people all over the world who, from the images and words that inundate us in the media, obviously don't think sex is a bad idea. With all this the child, though still not grasping all the issues, can accept the new idea into their world, confident the unknowns will be happily resolved at a later date.

To find God you follow the same process. Be content with some basic information to ease the uncertainties and, with that, make the plunge. That basic information can take many forms—it might be the assurance of a respected friend or identity who can say, "I've been there and it's good!" Or it might be the new understanding of where we came from— the Creator God (not a primordial soup and the vagaries of time and chance). Or perhaps the stark reality of divine interventions, miracles, fulfilled prophecies—things so hard to explain for the unbeliever, but pure common sense when you know a living God who is there. Or maybe the reality of millions of believers over centuries who, as they walked in the ways of God, enriched the world by serving the poor, fighting oppression, pioneering schools and hospitals, leading arts, music, and literature, and more—more than any other class of people, ever. The fact that many have even been willing to give their lives for their faith is a fair indicator they don't think God is a bad idea. There is ample witness, more than enough to put objections and unending questions on hold, trusting a good God will resolve them from a better vantage point at a later date.

Some might call this intellectual suicide, but to understand some things you need more than intellect. As I have said, intellect isn't enough to understand sex, nor is it enough to understand God. When I was wrestling with the idea of becoming a Christian, many objections leapt into my mind, but a little voice inside—I am sure it was God—answered them. But others reared their heads and I found myself procrastinating. At that point the little voice told me my demand for answers would never end in a field so vast, and I should stop trying to use them as excuses and take the step. From that vantage point—as a son of God with the Holy Spirit working in my life—I would learn far more easily. And that's how it worked out. You never stop learning as you walk with the glorious God. So join me, end the arguments, and step into the water.

So that's what the Bible says about sex between a man and a woman. But to finish the subject, what happens when, say, a homosexual meets God? Here is one story.

Chapter 17
THE GAY

A Love Story With a Difference
By Pastor Tom Gordon

"I have been charged for a homosexual act…I have been in jail for a short time…The court case is coming up…Will you marry me?"

What? Say that again? Was that true?

Yes, it was! This was where my life was at right then.

But you don't get to a point like that overnight. Where did it start?

I grew up in a country community in Victoria. Our farm was typical of the region—we grew wheat and raised sheep for their wool. Our life revolved around work on the farm and activities in our small town. My father was a great sportsman, an outdoorsman, who wanted me to follow in his footsteps, but I had no interest in sports. Where was the son he could play games with, teach the finer arts of cricket, instruct in riding a horse with the expected consummate skill? I was hopeless at team sports too, and it probably didn't help that there were only nine children in my primary school when I was eleven. Team sports were not really possible. I must have been a great disappointment to him. We were totally different people, and as time went on the gap between us grew ever wider. As a result our relationship was quite poor.

I was the eldest of four children. My sister, who was the next child, was quite sickly at birth and my mother had to spend a lot of time with her. I was left to my own devices and learned to be happy with my own company. My mother had been an artist before becoming a farmer's wife, and she encouraged me in my studies. Both my parents enjoyed reading, and as an avid reader, I found myself reading many books that were not intended for children.

When I was eleven, my father had a heart attack. He must have realized the seriousness of it, as he told me that if he died I would have to take over the farm. I could not imagine the rest of my life revolving round this kind of work. It was the last thing I would think of doing! So I prayed fervently for him to live, and he did—passing away eventually at the age of sixty-nine.

The motivation to pray for him came out of an experience I'd had as a small boy. A travelling evangelist called Dallas Clarnett came and spoke at a local hall. My parents had taken us along. I suppose they were invited and, as Dad was standing for Council, they went along for political reasons. My parents were definitely not in favor of "emotional" religion. My father's spiritual life revolved around the Masonic lodge.

However, the speaker talked about eternal life and asked for those who wanted this gift to come to the front of the church where he would pray for them. I felt God's call and really wanted to go forward. I knew it was right. But I was also very conscious that Dad and Mum would not approve. So I waited till we got home and I let my heart respond to the challenge. I wanted this eternal life! I knelt beside my bed and asked Jesus to come into my life. He came in, and I wanted to follow Him.

Two years before this, another primary school joined our little country school for a short period. It was hard at first to get used to having different children in the class, but they brought with them a most interesting but strange new game. It had to do with sex and was played between the boys and the girls. As young ones, we were forced to participate so we would not tell anyone. I was rather frightened by it, and confused. Of course we were found out, and my mother strongly told me I was not to touch a girl again. However, although I was confused by the games, I had already shared this secret sex play with some others, and while the games did not continue at school, they did continue with these other boys. The play intensified when I was sent to live with the family of these boys for a couple of years to be closer to a secondary school.

All this happened before I entered puberty. As a young boy I did not think about these games as being against God. I just knew they were naughty and were to be kept secret.

I could not wait to be old enough to leave home on a more permanent basis. My relationship with Dad had not improved. Looking back, I can see that he didn't know how to handle me. I think now that he probably loved me, but did not know how to show it. I felt rejected by him, as he often seemed angry with me, and I grew to despise him.

When I was seventeen I finally left home to study to become a teacher at the Ballarat Teachers College.

I immediately joined a church, as I still wanted to follow God. However, I was still very much aware that I was attracted to boys rather than girls. At college, to keep my desires a secret, I went out with girls now and then, but I fantasized and masturbated. I was caught up in this world. At times I even contemplated suicide. I felt so lonely with my secret and my questioning of my sexuality, which seemed so different from the world I saw about me. Some of the students noticed I was a bit different and oblique suggestions were made, but I denied their implications.

I was doing well academically and went to Melbourne for a third year, where I really enjoyed my life, kept attending church, and had several girlfriends. I found my faith was a good excuse for not having sex with anybody.

Over the years I was involved in attending church, Bible studies, youth groups, and other activities. I truly wanted to serve God.

However, in the 1960s, as I moved into my twenties, there were changes going on around the world. Ideas of freedom and a revolutionary spirit were moving among youth. I began to read existentialist writers like Camus and listen to the music of the late '60s and '70s, which talked of sex and change and loneliness and exploration. The conservatism of the world seemed stifling. I had friends fighting in Vietnam.

I had been called up but things were put off for years before I was finally rejected on medical grounds. I began to find church boring and started to drift away, embracing more of the hedonistic life of my friends. I was tempted more, but even though little happened I always felt extremely guilty. I knew that I was not living up to God's standards.

I received a job offer to work in Papua New Guinea. The job was to be in charge of all Education Department Libraries there. I decided to take it. The country was not yet self-governing, and I found myself with many responsibilities and away from friends, family, or restrictions. I thought of attending church but didn't, and was quite lonely over the first few months. Then as time went by and I had some negative experiences with women, I began to reach out to men for sex.

It was so easy. There were sexual partners every night. I spent a three-month vacation travelling Europe and had sexual experiences in many cities. I returned believing there was not a God. How could God have made me this way? Once I had made this decision, it was a relief. I was free to do anything. I began to drink a great deal. Sex obsessed my mind. I thought of little else, though I continued in my work and did well. Generally I came to know and love my partners in a shallow way, but all the time my heart was hardening, until sex was becoming an end in itself. I dabbled in the occult, experimenting with tarot cards. I believed that all I had was me, and, therefore, it did not matter what I did as long as I did not hurt anyone. I would go out and sometimes pick up five different guys in a night to take home for sex. I did not use protection and at times had to have medical attention. Fortunately AIDS was not yet on the scene.

One day when I was back in my office in Papua New Guinea, the police arrived and took me back to the lockup. Homosexuality was illegal in PNG. Someone had said something about me, and in my naivety I said things that confirmed their suspicions. I spent some hours in a cell before they charged and released me. I felt numb with shock. Going

home, I climbed a hill behind my house and cried out to that
God whom I had convinced myself did not exist.

"Help, God!" I called.

I could see my whole life disappearing. I would lose my job.
My friends would reject me. My sexuality had been a secret
because it was illegal. I would be in jail for years. I was full
of shame that my secret life was exposed, and full of fear of
the future.

However, my two-word prayer was enough to change
things. Amazing things began to happen. God began to put
in place a plan He had been working on well before I cried
out to Him.

There was a girl I knew—Joan. She was a strong Christian
and we had gone out together years before. I had even written
to her while I was travelling around Europe and told her I
was gay. I had not heard from her since I wrote. But I thought
we had a spark, and I needed to get out of this whole situation.
So I wrote to her again, explaining the mess I was in, and
asking her to come up to PNG and marry me. Maybe this
would help my case. I was clutching at straws in my distress,
but I now know God was in it.

I did not write with any great expectation, but Joan and I
had a strong friendship years before and I felt that whatever
happened I could share with her.

After some time, I received a letter from her saying she
was coming up to take a teaching position. Even before I had
written to her she had made these arrangements to come to
PNG.

So I greeted her at the airport with vague mumblings
about getting married. I wasn't really expecting much. It was
the vague hope of a numbed mind. She said to me, "I would
not consider marrying you until you were born again, baptized in water, and baptized in the Holy Spirit." Oh well!

I showed Joan around the town and she took me to the
Youth With A Mission (YWAM) headquarters, headed by a
young, rough-looking fellow named Tom. He took one look
at me and called me a heathen. I didn't mind, as I thought his

assessment of me was pretty accurate, and I liked his blunt approach.

Joan then left to take up her teaching position on Manus Island. Before she went she made me promise to go to church at least once. I promised.

After she had gone, on the following Sunday, I decided to go to the YWAM church, which met at night in a home. They ran a service at 6:00 p.m., as in Papua New Guinea the sun goes down at that time. I decided to go late, sneak in the back, and leave as soon as it finished. No one would see me or even know I was there.

When I pulled up at the house all was dark, and I wondered why. It seemed as though no one was there. But as I walked up, I noticed through the windows they were showing slides of mission work at Ukarumpa, the headquarters of Wycliffe Bible Translators in PNG. I was pleased, because it would make it easy to slip in the back door and sit down undetected. I was only going there to fulfill my promise to Joan.

So I walked quietly though the door, my eyes on the slide show. What I did not know was that some of the YWAM members on the base had little kids. To prevent them from crawling out into the night, they had erected a small barrier across the doorway.

In the gloom, I did not see it and walked straight into it. I tripped and literally flew into the room, crashing down full length on the floor with my breath knocked out of me. "Oomph!" People screamed and jumped out of their seats at this violent intrusion. Lights went on and everybody gathered to look at this gasping white man lying on the floor. They eventually helped me up and brought me forward to sit in the front row with the missionaries. So much for a back seat!

I allowed the service to wash over me, my arrogance totally drained out of me by my loud, clumsy entrance. Feeling humbled, I sensed the presence of God among these simple people. They were testifying of a God who provided, a God who cared, and of miracles that were happening. This was a living church, not a formal gathering of religious people. My heart was touched and I could not simply leave at the end of the service. I stayed for supper and talked to the people there. I knew I had reached a moment of decision, so I asked Tom and another leader to come and see me in my flat the next day.

They came and on that day—January 26, Australia Day, 1973—I told them my story, how I was caught up in homosexuality and had run afoul of the law. They had me pray a prayer of repentance and assured me that God had forgiven me. I felt a load was taken off my shoulders, and I was accepted by God. I had done a turnaround, and it felt good to be back where I could call myself a Christian.

I began attending services at YWAM, and the team encouraged me to be baptized in water. This would be the public declaration of my decision. The Saturday night before the baptism, one of my lovers came around and we commenced to have sex. I felt pulled in half and kept saying, "No! I can't do this. I am a Christian." As he left, I said, "Don't come back; I'm a Christian." I felt terrible. Any faith I possessed had been overpowered by my sexual desire.

Once I was alone, I fell to my knees in anguish and cried out, "I can't be baptized, I'm not good enough to be a Christian."

Waves of despair rolled over me, but suddenly I heard God's voice: "Who says you are not good enough? I love you!"

Immediately, I realized what had happened to me: "It was the devil telling me I am not good enough. He is the one who condemns and pulls down." So I determined to go ahead with the baptism. God had forgiven me and cleansed me from all the past.

The next day came. I rose, ready for my baptism.

The service was to be held on the beach at Gabutu. There were lots of people from the villages around, so it was a very public event. The YWAM team was playing guitars and singing, and I was given a megaphone to say why I was being baptized.

The water was very shallow, so we had to walk out a long

way. When it was my turn, I was asked if I would also like to receive the baptism in the Holy Spirit. Still feeling shattered by the experience of the previous evening, I said, "I need everything I can get to lead a Christian life."

So I was baptized, and came up out of the water speaking in tongues. I did not feel anything, but I suddenly had this language that I hadn't had before.

Only a week or so before, I had been talking to friends about the YWAM team and speaking in tongues. "They are very nice people," I said, "but no one is going to get me speaking that gibberish!" Now I spoke in tongues! I knew this was real, not gibberish! I knew it must be from God!

I had read the scripture from 1 Corinthians 14:4, "He who speaks in [an unknown] tongue edifies himself" (NKJV), so I determined to speak in a tongue whenever I had the opportunity, to build myself up in the faith. A week or so later, driving my car and speaking in tongues, I had an experience that seemed to go through my body like a rushing wind. It was a cleansing, purifying feeling. I felt like I was a battery that had just been recharged and the light came on.

My worship and life were now more in tune with God.

Joan agreed to marry me, and we became engaged. I was amazed to learn that God had spoken to Joan about this three years previously, just after I moved to PNG. He told her we would marry, even giving her the date, which she wrote in the margin of her Bible: "21/9/70—3 years"! (She still has that Bible.) How that date was fulfilled was also amazing. Because Joan was teaching, we had to marry during school holidays. Providentially she was placed at Waigani Primary, the only school in PNG that had its holidays on our date, September 21! This was an experimental school set up by the university and its holidays followed the university semester year instead of the three terms of government schools.

I then wrote to Joan's father, who was aware of the situation, formally asking his blessing on marrying his daughter. He was a wonderful Christian man. In his response to me he quoted the scripture, "If anyone is in Christ, he is a new creation; old things have passed away; behold, all things have become new" (2 Cor. 5:17, nkjv). I wept.

Our honeymoon in Tapini was wonderful. My desire was for my wife. My addiction to the same sex was broken. God continued to do great things. I did not go to jail or lose my job; and in 1976, back in Australia, our first child was born. God is an amazing God!

Although I still have some same-sex attraction, its power over me is broken, and I dedicated my life to serving God, His church, and my family.

One of the hardest things I had to do was share my story with my children. I waited until the youngest was almost a teenager. It was a shock to them. But my son said, "That's good, Dad. You will be able to help other people." That was the reason I told them, so that I would be free to help others who were struggling with same-sex attraction and their faith. I now speak at various churches, encouraging those who struggle with same-sex attraction to stick with Jesus.

I have been a pastor for nearly thirty years and ministered in many countries. I have been happily married for thirty-nine years, and have three married children and (at the moment) seven grandchildren. Now in my midsixties, I still see God doing amazing things in my life. He is my Lord, and I continue to serve Him.

I know that I was rescued from death. AIDS was just moving into the country when I left a lifestyle of unprotected sex. I sit with all my family members, all going on with God, and I bless God that although I turned away from Him, He never turned away from me. He intervened in my life, restoring me to my proper place as His son.

I can vouch for Tom and Joan. They have been close friends for decades and their children grew up with ours and remain friends today. The favor of God on the family is substantial.

Of course, there are many people like Tom who can tell stories of God at work in their lives, healing sexual issues and getting them on track. God has a miracle for everyone, for every concern life throws our way. Sometimes the miracle comes in the form of a message—a message from heaven. The effect of a message from heaven can be just as profound as a physical miracle, as you will see in this next section.

SECTION 4: HEAVEN

Chapter 18
THE BOY WHO WENT TO HEAVEN
And Launched a New York Times *Best Seller*

S TRANGE THINGS HAD been happening in the Burpo family, but what got Todd Burpo wondering if his four-year-old, Colton, might have been to heaven was his sheepish response when reprimanded for not sharing toys: "Yeah, I know, Dad. Jesus told me I had to be nice."[1]

Jesus told him? Where did that come from?

Other things followed. Like when they drove past the hospital where Colton had almost died and they asked if he remembered the place. He replied, "'Yes...that's where the angels sang to me.'

"'What did they sing to you?'

"'Well they sang "Jesus Loves Me" and "Joshua Fought the Battle of Jericho," he said earnestly. 'I asked them to sing "We Will, We Will Rock You," but they wouldn't sing that.[2] ...Jesus had the angels sing to me because I was so scared. They made me feel better.'

"'Well where was Jesus?'

"'I was sitting on Jesus' lap.'"[3]

And that's just the beginning of the revelations of this book, *Heaven Is for Real.* The touching anecdotes struck a chord with multitudes of readers, and hurtled the book to number one on the *New York Times* Best Seller List.

It's not as though Colton comes from a wacky family. His father is a Wesleyan minister in a small town in Nebraska. If you want a solid, theologically conservative denomination that shuns all that is flaky, you probably can't go past the Wesleyans. And to help support his family, Colton's dad runs a business fitting garage doors; his wife is a qualified teacher from the public schools system. Everything about them shouts, "These are not weird people!"

But things had gone wrong in the Burpo household. Todd shattered his leg in a softball game; then he developed kidney stones;

then a lump in his chest (hyperplasia) required a rare operation for men—a mastectomy.

After all that, Colton developed a ruptured appendix that lay undiscovered for days, and he was not expected to live. After a long ordeal in getting the diagnosis right, desperate surgery to clean him out, and frantic prayer, Colton miraculously recovered. It was such a surprise that hospital staff would come into his room to stare at him. A nurse even took Todd aside, acknowledging the recovery as a miracle, and telling Todd staff had been instructed not to give encouragement to the family, as they fully believed Colton would die.

After all this, every now and then Colton would spill out more stories of his time in heaven. Here are just a few:

- Colton: "Daddy, remember when I yelled for you in the hospital when I waked up?...Well the reason I was yelling was that Jesus came to get me. He said I had to go back because He was answering your prayer. That's how come I was yelling for you."[4]

- When Todd asked Colton what Jesus looked like, he said, "Jesus has markers. And He has brown hair and He has hair on His face" [demonstrating a beard], "And His eyes...oh, Dad, His eyes are so pretty!"[5] Asked what he meant by "markers"—did he mean the ones he used for coloring in pictures, and if so, what color were they—Colton replied: "Yeah...Red, Daddy. Jesus has red markers on Him."[6] When Todd asked where the markers were, Colton simply pointed to the palms of his hands and the tops of his feet.

- Todd was preparing for a funeral and Colton asked him about the man who had died. His father writes: Colton "stared fiercely into my eyes. 'Did the man have Jesus in his heart?...He *had* to know Jesus or he can't get into heaven!'"[7] Later, at the funeral, nearly in tears, Colton yelled, "He had to know Jesus, Dad!"[8] He created such a scene they had to keep him away from funerals after that time.

- Colton, to his mother Sonja:

    "Mommy, I have two sisters"...

    "No, you have your sister, Cassie, and...do you mean your cousin, Traci?"

    "No." Colton clipped off the word adamantly. "I have two *sisters*. You had a baby die in your tummy didn't you?"...

    "Who told you I had a baby die in my tummy?"

    "She did, Mommy. She said she died in your tummy."[9]

    Then Colton went on to describe how he had met the sister he had never even heard about, the sister who was miscarried before Colton was born. The poignant details of this story give a whole new insight into issues of life and eternity. The book is worth reading just for this section.

- Colton had never seen his grandfather—he died twenty-five years before Colton was born. So Todd was surprised when Colton said he met him in heaven. He showed Colton his grandfather's photo, taken just before he died at age sixty-one. But Colton showed no signs of recognition, and frowned, explaining that in heaven nobody is old or wears glasses. Later they dug out the grandfather's photo as a young man of twenty-nine, and without comment showed it to Colton. Eyes full of surprise he asked happily, "How did you get a picture of Pop?"[10]

- Todd asked Colton had he seen Satan. He had, but would explain no more. Todd said, "Colton's body went rigid, he grimaced, and his eyes narrowed to a squint."[11] And he would say no more that night.

- On another occasion Colton asked his father if he knew there was going to be a war, and then went on to describe what he had seen.

And there is much more.

Throughout the book Todd links many of Colton's experiences with the Bible. Things he had been too young to understand or had never learned matched exactly with Bible stories.

God has stepped into our world to speak to us through a child.
As the Bible says:

> A little child shall lead them.
>
> —Isaiah 11:6, NKJV

> From the lips of children and infants you have ordained praise.
>
> —Matthew 21:16, NIV1984

Colton's experience is certainly unusual, way out there. Here is another. It touches on two issues. Firstly, the Bible talks a lot about angels. Are they real? If so what do they do? Where are they today? Secondly, can God enter the world of the intellectually disabled? Here is an amazing story.

Chapter 19
THE DISABLED SON

By Rebekah Milne

My son, Matthew, is a very talkative, intellectually disabled thirty-three-year-old. Highly social, he is constantly looking for an opportunity to talk with anyone about anything. Matthew is a gentle giant; he wouldn't hurt a fly. His favorite pastime is to find anyone to answer his never-ending questions.

One day Matt was at his life skills training program and one of the clients became so angry with Matt's persistent questioning that he said he was going to stab him. Besieged by fear, Matt tried to defend himself by saying, "Mum won't let you." But the angry peer said, "I will sneak into your house while your parents are asleep and they will never know, but you will be dead in the morning."

Matt had a severe breakdown. He couldn't leave the house, and became obsessed with the idea that he had done something wrong and police were coming to get him. He would rock and cry about having to go out. He couldn't sleep at night, and was crying and constantly asking if some minor act of his was going to bring the police to our door to arrest him. If he saw a police car while I was driving him somewhere he would begin rocking in fear.

The family was very stressed because nothing we said could settle him or ease his anxiety. Eventually we found a medication to use when panic attacks grabbed him, and it helped him sleep.

When revival came to our church, Diggerland, Matthew began to pray for his own healing. He attended every prayer meeting, and at every meeting he asked God to heal him.

One morning before church, Matthew came to me in the bathroom and said he didn't sleep much the night before.

I asked him why, and he said, "The angels came to my room." I thought he was saying he had a dream but he emphatically insisted it was not a dream; angels had come into his room over his bed.

I asked what they looked like—he said they were shining and white. So I asked what they did or said. He ran off to his room to get something and came back with a scrap of paper with baby-like scrawl on it. It read: "2 Timothy 1:5–7."

So I asked how he was able to write this scripture reference. Matthew can't read, and can only write by copying something set in front of him. He said, "The angel put the words on my head and told me to write it down." That was most surprising to me. Nothing like it had ever happened before.

I asked did the angels say anything else. He replied, "Yes. He said, 'God has not given me a spirit of fear but love power and a sound mind.'" Matt wouldn't know that the verse he was quoting was the scripture reference on the piece of paper.

From that minute on Matt was healed. He required no more medication and he had no more fear.

But the following Monday it was tested.

There was another incident at the Skills Training Program, and the workers called me, very concerned. One of the clients had grabbed Matt in a headlock and punched him. The workers apologized profusely, particularly given what Matt had been through recently. So they brought him home, and I held my breath as he walked through the door.

"Hi, Mum," he said. "Joe had a bad day today. Oh well, we all have bad days. What's for dinner?"

I sighed a great sigh of relief. It was done.

Praise God!

THERE IS MORE to this story.

Matthew's mother, Rebekah Milne, and her husband, Glenn, have seven children (one of whom is adopted), and two more of the boys have a disability similar to that of Matt. This has been a severe trial for Glenn and Rebekah for many years and a tremendous test of their faith.

Rebekah Milne is also a pastor at their church, Diggerland, in Red Cliffs, Victoria, Australia. Active in counseling and preaching, she occasionally makes ministry trips to Mexico and other developing countries, preaching and praying for the sick and demonized. Many extraordinary miracles have occurred in these times. She is a woman of great faith.

That faith is the stamp of her family. Her parents are Cliff and Helen Beard, Australian pioneering evangelists, a couple with extraordinary faith who for decades have preached the gospel, planted churches, witnessed miracles, established orphanages and other care for the needy in developing countries. So Rebekah shares their mantle, and in particular that of her mother, Helen, who pioneered women's ministry in many areas of Australia and overseas. It's easy to understand that Matthew's faith, the faith that drove him to all the prayer meetings to overcome his fear, is a natural by-product of that family background.

When you look at the rest of 2 Timothy 1:5–7, which Matthew wrote down, everything else comes relevant to this story. (Matthew quoted only a part of it, as above.) Here is the whole passage where the apostle Paul is addressing young Timothy:

> [I remember] the genuine faith that is in you, which dwelt first in your grandmother Lois and your mother Eunice, and I am persuaded is in you also. Therefore I remind you to stir up the gift of God which is in you through the laying on of my hands. For God has not given us a spirit of fear, but of power and of love and of a sound mind.
>
> —2 Timothy 1:5–7, nkjv

Matt's problem was fear, and the verse he quoted dealt with that. The reference to the faith of the grandmother and mother puts it into context; Matt inherited a great faith from his family, and the angel reminded him that he also has that faith.

What an amazing thing that Matthew should venture out that morning, with a story of angels, with a verse he wrote on a piece of paper (when he can't do that!), with such specific reference to his situation, leading to his complete healing from that terrible, irrational fear! God is so good!

This next miracle from heaven is in a field where you might not expect miracles—music. Music plays a huge role in our lives. We tend to forget we are made in the image of God, and music is a spin-off from that association. So we shouldn't be surprised to find God rolling up His sleeves and getting involved in songwriting.

Chapter 20
THE SONGWRITER

By Nolene Prince

"Would the lady who was conducting the choir please come up here."

I was startled by the request in front of six or seven hundred people, but obediently stood up from my seat several rows back and walked forward.

The preacher was evangelist Dick Mills. I'm not sure the title "evangelist" exactly fit him. He had an unusual ministry that had emerged after he memorized over a thousand verses from the Bible—verses relating to promises of God. He found that when he prayed for people, verses would spring to his mind—helpful verses, related to issues in the person's life, of which he knew nothing. The effect was often dramatic, and many people had been helped immensely. So he was more a prophet than an evangelist; but I think the title "prophet" would spook a few people, and that's probably why he chose "evangelist."

It was the last night of a week of public meetings with Dick Mills, and we had seen his remarkable gift operating multiple times, so I wondered what he had for me. Happily all his words were recorded and we still have a copy. This is what he said:

When you were up there leading, the Lord spoke to me by a word of knowledge, indicating that He is going to give you an original song—a song that will be easily sung by masses of people. Also, it will be a song that will be easily translated into other languages. Have you ever written music? Yes? OK... a song that will bless the church... You're going to get this song when you're in bed, isn't that something?...

At this point he quoted several scriptures, including Psalm 32:7: "You are my hiding place; you will protect me from trouble and surround me with songs of deliverance," and Psalm 149:5: "Let his faithful people rejoice in this honor and sing for joy on their beds." He said the song would come from the scriptures and I would take the words and make them rhyme.

Four very specific things! It seemed impossible. A song that would bless the church, be easily sung, translatable into other languages, and written in bed! I had composed a few songs to that point; but while some went quite well, none had been wildly successful, none had shown promise for translation, and certainly none had been written in bed. I always worked at the piano, with one hand on the keys, the other with pen and paper.

Nevertheless, I dutifully placed a pen and manuscript paper on the bedside table. After all, faith without works is dead! And I really don't like getting out of bed!

At about 10:00 p.m., I was in bed reading Isaiah 6:

In the year that King Uzziah died, I saw the Lord, high and exalted, seated on a throne; and the train of his robe filled the temple. Above him were seraphim, each with six wings: With two wings they covered their faces, with two they covered their feet, and with two they were flying. And they were calling to one another:

"Holy, holy, holy is the LORD Almighty; the whole earth is full of his glory."

—Verses 1–3

I began to picture the scene Isaiah was describing—the throne, its glory, and the worshipping seraphim. As I did I could hear in my mind something of the melody they were singing, so I picked up the pen and paper and wrote it down.

A few minutes later my husband, Dennis, came in. I told him I had just written a song. He said he had just found a good verse for a song, and asked where mine was from. To our amazement, it was the identical passage from Isaiah 6! It was pure "coincidence"—we had not been intentionally following the same readings at all.

We sang the song "Holy Is the Lord of Hosts" at our church and taught it in several other places around the country. People loved to worship God through it. But we said nothing of the prophecy, happy to let God do what He wanted without pushing the issue. Months later I sent a copy to David and Dale Garratt in New Zealand. They were well known for songbooks they had produced called *Scripture in Song* and had already used a couple of my other songs. I told them nothing of the prophecy I had received.

A year or so later David phoned me on some copyright issues. He told me they had travelled to several countries teaching worship and that "Holy Is the Lord of Hosts" had been very popular. They had even included it in an album they recorded in French! Excited by that piece of information, I told him of the prophecy. David then related to me about some meetings they had conducted for Christian gatherings at the Montreal Olympic Games. The visitors and athletes from many countries sang the song together, translating it into their various languages.

Since then we have heard multiple stories of the song in other countries. A friend was in a German church, not understanding a word of the service, when to his delight they began singing the song in German. We received a book published in Chinese that contained the song, and another in Japanese. A request came in to use it in a South African songbook in Afrikaans. A well-known missionary movie, *The Wait of the World,* included a scene in a small church in South America with the people singing "Holy Is the Lord of Hosts" in Spanish. It has been used in Holland and in Russia. And there are many others we have lost track of.

Dennis and I went on to publish our own praise and worship songbooks, with compilations of the best songs we could find from all over the world. They were widely used by several thousand churches around Australia. I usually included one of my own songs with each new release, and over the years

I probably wrote fifty more songs, some of which became quite popular. But none gained the worldwide popularity of "Holy Is the Lord of Hosts," and none was birthed from a specific prophecy in the same way. As I write this, almost four decades later, we still receive significant royalties from its use around the world—a tangible measure that the church is still being blessed by singing it.

It was truly a song from heaven, a miracle from God.

The song, the story, and the recording of the original prophecy can be found on YouTube—just google *Song from Heaven—Nolene Prince.*

So a man predicted the future. That is the stamp of God. We don't have power to foretell the future—it has to be divine. Is there more of it in God's dealings with people? Is it in the Bible? What about fortune-telling? Look at this next section.

Chapter 21

THE FUTURE

Can It Be Told?

IF YOU WANT to know the future, God tells us to ask only Him.
Don't look elsewhere (Isa. 8:19). Horoscopes, fortune-tellers,
spiritism, and all other things related to the occult are out.
When it comes to predicting the future God is unequalled. He lives
outside time and He knows everything. From that perspective He
has proven Himself multiple times.

For instance, the Old Testament accurately foretold hundreds of
things about cities, rulers, and the coming Messiah, Jesus Christ. It
would take many pages to detail them all, but here are just a few.

About 750 BC, God's prophet Ezekiel (chapter 26) had some
words for the city of Tyre, which sat on the coastline of Palestine.
He declared that its fortresses would fall, its stones and timbers
would be thrown into the sea, it would be made a bare rock, a place
for fishermen to dry their nets, and it would never be rebuilt. That's
a bold prophecy. Imagine telling the world those things were all
going happen to New York. But it all happened to Tyre about 333
BC, just as prophesied. An army attacked it, the people fled to an
island offshore, and the army built a causeway to the island with
the stones and timber of the buildings. It was stripped bare, and
fishermen dried their nets there, exactly as God said. You can get
the full story on Bible prophecy websites.

Other prophecies include the destruction of Edom (or Petra) in
Obadiah chapter 1; the curse on Babylon (Isa. 13); the destruction of
Nineveh (Nah. 1–3); and the return of Israel to the land (Isa. 11:11).
All happened just as God said. Again, go to Bible prophecy websites
for more.

Much information was also given about the coming of Jesus
Christ, centuries before He was born. Here are just a few: His place
of birth (Bethlehem) in Micah 5:2; He would enter Jerusalem on a
donkey (Zech. 9:9); He would be betrayed for thirty pieces of silver

(Zech. 11:12–13); He would be wounded and bruised (Isa. 53:5; see also 50:6); He would be mocked (Ps. 22:7–8); His hands and feet would be pierced (on the cross) (Ps. 22:16 and Zech. 12:10); He would be rejected (Isa. 53:3); lots would be cast for His clothes (Ps. 22:18); and much more. You can even calculate the date of Christ's first coming in Daniel chapter 9. That is remarkable! Fulfilled prophecy runs throughout the Bible and is a clear indicator of God's authority.

Is there more prophecy still waiting to happen? Does the Bible predict what will happen to the world? Certainly. Here are some world events waiting in the wings. Just remember, the order of events is not always clear—it will be fully obvious only after it all happens.

We can expect:

- Normal activities—eating and drinking and marrying—before a sudden, *unexpected* end (Luke 17)

- Signs in the sun, moon, and stars, and roaring and tossing of the sea (Luke 21)

- Massive financial collapse (Rev. 18)

- Middle East war (Ezek. 38–39)

- Earth's final destiny (2 Pet. 3:1–13)

- The final things and eternity (Rev. 20–21; Isa. 11)

Fulfilled prophecy in the Bible tells us two things: first that the Bible is valid—it is God's word to us; and second, we can read about tomorrow today and know where we are headed.

So heaven spoke—to a small boy named Colton, to a young man with a disability, to a songwriter, and to prophets in the Bible over many centuries. All these are the stamp of a loving holy God who, through His Son Jesus, speaks to His children on a plethora of different issues.

Does this happen in other religions? Is God at work there? Read this next section for some unexpected answers.

SECTION 5: RELIGION

Chapter 22
THE HINDU GURU

A FEW WEEKS AFTER marrying his fifteen-year-old bride, a devout Hindu named Chandrabhan Ragbir Sharma Mahabir Maharaj made some mysterious secret religious vows. As a result of these vows he abandoned all work and social interaction, dedicating himself to reading the sacred scriptures and meditating. The vows were drastic and life changing. For eight years until his death he spoke to no one, not even his wife. Most of his time was spent in a trancelike state. People recognized his remarkable "achievement" and flocked to worship him. Seated in lotus position on his board, his mind far away, he would not even acknowledge them. After his death he was declared by some to be an avatar, a god in human form.

After his marriage and in the few weeks before taking his secret vows, his wife conceived their only child, a boy named Rabindranath. As he grew up, Rabindranath earnestly wanted his father to speak to him, to acknowledge him, even once; but it never happened. In spite of this, from the age of five, young Rabindranath showed by his unusual devotion that he would follow in his father's footsteps. Fortune-tellers, palm readers and astrologers predicted he would become a great Hindu leader—a Yogi or guru, pundit, sanyasi, or perhaps a temple high priest. While other children played, he read the sacred scriptures, practiced yoga, or worshipped and cared for his beloved sacred cow.

Because of his rapid progress and his father's reputation, at age eleven he entered the temple for a time under the guidance of a brilliant priest.

In visions and trances, remarkable supernatural things happened: he experienced unearthly music, saw psychedelic colors, visited exotic planets, talked to gods, and saw the horrible demonic creatures depicted by the images in Hindu, Buddhist, Shinto and other religious temples. His experiences were frightening but real. The head priest was delighted with Rabindranath's rapid progress.

He continued to advance and was widely acclaimed. Though only a boy, he had scaled the heights of Hinduism. People came to worship him, to receive his blessing. They would bring money and gifts to his feet. He enjoyed the adulation.

Yet many things troubled young Rabindranath, though he would never admit his doubts to anyone.

- He had been taught self-denial but found some students at the temple to be gluttons. Furthermore, the young head priest, though sworn to celibacy, had a continuous affair with a beautiful young girl. The people condoned his actions with the explanation, "It's karma. They have something from their last life to work out together."[1] (For the Hindu, karma is the law of cause and effect. Experiences in this life are the consequences of actions in past lives. Each person suffers for past deeds; there is no forgiveness.)

- Although he was meticulous about his vegetarianism (he wouldn't even buy cheese if the cutting knife had been used on meat), he smoked heavily, in secret, and couldn't give it up. He wouldn't buy cigarettes in case someone saw him, so he stole them, and this tormented his conscience even more. No matter how hard he prayed he seemed to be losing the battle in his soul.

- For several years, each day for an hour, he would worship his beloved cow. Then one day it turned on him violently for no reason, and he barely escaped death or serious injury. As he looked back at the angrily pawing hoofs and the hatred in its eyes, he pondered: why would his god attack him when he had worshipped and cared for it with such devotion? Shiva and Kali and so many of the other gods often frightened him, but the cow was one god he had adored.

- In his Yogic trances he frequently met the god Shiva—known as the Destroyer—always in a seated position with a huge cobra round his neck hissing menacingly. He wondered why none of the gods he encountered seemed kind and loving. He comforted himself with the thought that at least they were real, not myths like the Christian god Santa Claus.

- Household family arguments were bitter and frequent. He was troubled that he could so quickly turn from the bliss of a long meditation to a state of anger and rage. Sometimes he would take a whiplike branch and lash at a concrete pillar till he was exhausted, then stand wondering what had gotten into him. Once he took a strap, which he often used to beat the family, and lashed it repeatedly across the backs of several of his younger girl cousins, then retreated in confusion and shame.

- His non-Hindu fellow school students taunted him and mocked his beliefs. If *everything* is a god, did that mean his god is a fly, an ant, a *stinkbug*? And if he believed all life was sacred and would not eat animals, what about the bacteria he killed when he boiled water? His answers, such as, "You only see the illusion but don't see the One Reality—Brahman"[2] were powerless, and he wondered about the need for his faith to be practical.

- Some "holy" men, for a fee, would bless lottery tickets. When the people didn't win and asked why not, they were told, "It's your karma." The holy man became rich and the people stayed poor.

- A frail old holy man once came to Rabindranath asking for food. This was common practice, so he obliged. He also assisted the man to the toilet, though he was filthy and his body and long, matted hair smelt revolting. He felt good about helping the man but was astonished when, for all his kindness, he received a torrent of filthy abuse for not renouncing his possessions and embracing poverty as the holy man had done. Was that right? Certainly he had been taught poverty was more spiritual; riches were part of the illusion of ignorance. Yet one of the gods they were taught to worship was Lakshmi, goddess of wealth and prosperity! Furthermore, when he considered the philosophy of karma and the promise of progress to higher things through reincarnation, and then looked at the darkness and poverty in India, the home of Hinduism, he saw only bitter contradiction. Thousands of years of Yoga, improving karma, and upward reincarnation toward oneness with Brahman had brought nothing but abject poverty. Why was he so reluctant to acknowledge this? Was he afraid of the truth?

- His deeply spiritual Hindu mother had once advised him: "If you are ever in trouble and nothing else seems to work, there is another god you can pray to. His name is Jesus."[3] One day he was walking through beautiful vegetation, admiring the flowers and birds, when a huge, thick snake confronted him, remarkably like the one coiled around the neck of his god Shiva. Paralyzed by fear, he could not flee; a sheer rock wall lay behind him. Close enough to touch, the snake drew back its head to strike. Remembering the words of his mother, in desperation he cried, "Jesus, help me!" To his utter astonishment, the snake dropped to the ground, turned around, and slithered off rapidly into the jungle. Trembling with shock, he was filled with gratitude to this amazing God Jesus, astonished he had never learned anything about Him at a Christian primary school he once attended.

- On another occasion he had his appendix removed—a close call, it had almost burst. Feeling better on the third day, he was allowed to go to the toilet alone. But, on returning, an excruciating pain struck his right side, and the room began to swim. Remembering his mother's words and the snake incident, he cried out again, "Jesus, help me!" Though no one was there he felt a hand grip his arm, and the darkness lifted, every twinge of pain vanished, and a remarkable feeling of well-being surged through him. A strange calm descended on the room and he fell into a deep sleep. When he woke, a Christian tract lay on his bedside table, the first he had ever seen. It moved him deeply. But with so many other gods to worship, he forgot it.

- He was torn between two irreconcilable views. One was an instinct he had since a child that God was *separate* and *distinct* from the universe He had made.[1*] The other was the Hindu teaching that god (Brahman) *was everything*; creation and creator were one and the same. His experiences in meditation agreed with the second view, but after hours in a trance it was difficult to face the everyday world of joys and sorrows and the conflicts they brought.

- He had been taught that there was only one Reality. Did this mean the Brahman was evil as well as good, death as well as life, hatred as well as love? That made everything meaningless, life an absurdity. Furthermore, if good and evil were the same, then all karma was the same and nothing mattered. So, why be religious? Whenever he asked his teachers such questions, the answer was, "Reason cannot be trusted—it is part of the illusion." He was not satisfied.

- Once, in a blind rage, he turned on his aunt when she accused him of being lazy, "Just like your father."[4] Scarcely conscious of his actions he grabbed a set of barbell weights, and swung it like a baseball bat at his aunt, aiming for her head. But his frantic cousin managed to grab the other end and the weights fell, smashing the thick concrete. All three were stunned. Rabin ran to his room, locked the door, and cried for hours. He had preached nonviolence; he would not even step on an ant—such was his respect for life. How could he have done this terrible thing? And how did he manage to lift the heavy weights? At night he crept out to check the barbells—he could not even raise them off the ground. Who were these strong gods he had invited into himself? Would it happen again? He stayed in his room for days, emerging eventually to a very tense household.

- Approaching fifteen, he was greatly disturbed by an experience at a puja conducted in his home. This was a ceremony

---

1   * Instinct: No doubt the instinct mentioned in Romans 1:19–20: "Since what may be known about God is plain to them, because God has made it plain to them. For since the creation of the world God's invisible qualities—his eternal power and divine nature—have been clearly seen, being understood from what has been made, so that people are without excuse."

where people came to worship him and place gifts at his feet. Many people came with respectful bows, speaking with glowing terms of the fame this Yogi would one day bring to their town. A poor widow placed a number of coins at his feet—more than a month's earnings. The gods had decreed that people should bring gifts to Yogis in this way and the Vedas (Hindu scriptures) taught it would greatly benefit the giver, so there was no need to feel guilt. But as the poor lady awaited his blessing, Rabindranath was "startled by a voice of unmistakable omnipotent authority: 'You are not God, Rabi!'"[5] He began to tremble, knowing instantly the true God had spoken and the "blessing" he was about to bestow on the lady was fraudulent.

- He rushed to his room, where he stayed, not eating for four days, agonizing, praying, weeping, and grappling with the realization of his sins and the foolishness of the idea that a cow, a snake, or even he, could be a god. Once on the "verge of Self-realization,"[6] he now grovelled in abject self-condemnation. He knew his good works could never outweigh his bad, and trembled at the thought of reincarnation, certain his karma would drop him to the bottom of the ladder. He tried to find God by the only means he knew, looking inside himself, but this only stirred up a nest of evil. If he couldn't find God he felt he must commit suicide, but then retreated, with the thought that his next life could be even worse.

Soon after this pivotal experience, a girl from his school came and told him about Jesus Christ and how He had brought her peace. Struck by her obvious happiness, he talked with her for nearly half a day. He was stunned by the idea that God could be a God of love. Then, after days of the worst turmoil and conflict he had ever known, he finally and reluctantly concluded that the darkness in his heart could never be changed by thousands of holy baths, pujas, and yoga. So he prayed a desperate and difficult prayer: "God, the true God and Creator, please show me the *Truth!* Please, God!"[7] Something snapped inside him, and for the first time in his life he felt he had prayed and gotten through.

After overcoming a few more hurdles, he eventually attended a small Christian gathering at the invitation of his cousin. There he was overwhelmed by the joy, the love and praise for God, by the knowledge that righteousness was a gift and could not be earned. Responding to an invitation from the preacher (a former Muslim—"one of the worst rowdies"[8] he had known from his primary school days), he asked Jesus into his life. He became totally new inside, knowing peace for the first time. He said:

> I wept tears of repentance for the way I had lived: for the anger and hatred and selfishness and pride, for the idols I had served, for accepting the worship that belonged to God alone, and for imagining that *He* was like a cow or a star or a man....tons of darkness seemed to lift and a brilliant light flooded my soul[9]....How wonderfully different from reincarnation was resurrection. The slate was wiped clean, and I eagerly looked forward to the new life I had begun in Jesus, my Lord.[10]

Immediately he threw away his cigarettes, having lost all desire for them. He apologised to his aunt for his bad behavior. Forgiveness, not being part of karma and the Hindu faith, had been absent from his family life until then. The whole household became Christians. Free from the fear that had once bound them, they piled up their idols and religious pictures and burned them. There was "no compromise, no possible blending of Hinduism and true Christianity. They were diametrically opposed." They hugged one another with joy, singing praises to God. "The evil powers could terrorize us no longer,"[11] Rabindranath said.

The transformation in the household was dramatic. The bitter arguments were now a thing of the past. Rabindranath began to help with the chores. The teenagers all pitched in to transform the garden, to the wondering looks of neighbors. His paralyzed grandmother, who had failed to respond to the best medical experts and the highest-paid Hindu healers, was healed through prayer. And the house that had been haunted for years by strange noises, mysterious footsteps, disagreeable odors, and moving objects was now at peace. All who had lived or stayed there had witnessed these frightening activities—now they were gone.

At school his friends now began to persecute him for his Christian faith, even the boys he had thought were Christians. It became unbearable, and one night he was particularly discouraged, asking God why it was so difficult to be a Christian. At about 2:00 a.m., someone clothed in a bright white light woke him up, shaking him. The figure held out his hand and said softly, "Peace! My peace I give to you!" then vanished. Rabindranath knew it was Jesus, and he gained new courage from the experience and a new assurance that Jesus would be guiding and caring for him.

Subsequently, he went to Europe and worked with drug addicts and young people on their way to investigate the religions of India. He was astonished to find their drug-induced hallucinatory experiences were identical to those he had experienced in meditation, and recognized demonic forces behind them.

At a lecture at Harvard University he was once asked, "You have turned from Hinduism to Christianity. How would you react to someone in your present position who turns to your former position?" He replied, "I would *never* be able to understand how anyone in my present position could ever turn back to my former position if he were *really* in my present position. From my observation, the Westerners who are turning to the East simply never knew Christ personally."[12]

The full story of Rabindranath is told in his book *Death of a Guru*.

A story like that unsettles comfortable views about other faiths, and the politically correct way we approach the subject. But it inevitably raises the question, What about other religions? What about Muslims, for example? Here is a story that is so remarkable it sounds like fiction.

Chapter 23
THE MUSLIM

A Modern-Day Thriller with a Difference

H E WAS THE eldest son of Sheikh Hassan Yousef, one of seven founders of Hamas, the Palestinian terrorist organization. Always by his father's side, privy to information at the highest level, his father trusted him more than any other person. Then, to the astonishment of family and fellow Palestinians, he sought asylum in the United States. There the U.S. Department of Homeland Security tried to deport him. But twenty-one members of Congress signed a letter to support his application for asylum. And former director of the CIA R. James Woolsley said his deportation "would be such an inhumane act it would constitute a blight on American history."[1]

What happened? What caused the remarkable turnaround?

The answer is a story that reads like a modern spy thriller and strips away the shrouds of confusion that dog the Palestinian/Israeli conflict. All is told in a book: *Son of Hamas*, by Mosab Hussein Yousef, a *New York Times* best seller.

The background to the Israeli/Palestinian conflict has a huge bearing on the story, and the book explains it well.

From its commencement in AD 1517, Islam spread across three continents sweeping all before it. But after a few centuries of great economic and political power, the system became centralized and corrupt. Persecution and crushing taxation led to decline, and many of the disillusioned turned to atheism or communism, or succumbed to alcohol, gambling, or porn from the West. In 1928, a new movement arose, the Muslim Brotherhood, which blamed the West for its ills, saying the only hope was a return to the purity and simplicity of Islam. It preached a side of Islam not known to the West, a side reflecting mercy, education and welfare, and the poor responded with warmth and loyalty. This was the face of the early Muslim Brotherhood. (MB)

In 1948 the MB took up arms in an unsuccessful coup against the secular Egyptian government, and then joined the Arab resistance against the new Jewish state of Israel. By the midseventies the MB was greatly loved, as it encouraged the faith, healed hurts, and improved lives. Mosab's father, Hassan, was a keen supporter of the movement. A young man at that time, he was working on his studies, following in his own father's footsteps to be an Imam.

Mosab's father, Sheik Hassan Yousef, is a key character throughout the book, and Mosab consistently expresses the highest regard for him. Time after time he interrupts the story to sing his father's praise and unfold his qualities. To name a few: Hassan loved his wife, demonstrating his love in many ways. He helped with household work, even washing his own socks. He was devoted to his flock; many a night he returned home late, having been mediating in arguments, helping the unfortunate, or conducting a funeral. Though exhausted from his work, he would still make time to pray and cry out to Allah. While other Palestinian leaders drove $70,000.00 cars, his was a modest 1987 Audi. When imprisoned and tortured by the Israelis he shared his food with his jailers, who came to love him. When Mosab wanted revenge against the Israelis, Hassan taught him not to be racist but "be good to your mother…to Allah, and…to people."[2] Mosab said, "He was my everything, my example of what it means to be a man…such an example of humility, love, and devotion; even though he was only five foot seven, he stood head and shoulders above anyone else I had ever known."[3]

So Sheik Hassan continued his work for the people and his support for the MB, and became a popular Imam in a deprived and overcrowded refugee camp. Many of the young people pressured the MB to stand against the Israelis. "Doesn't the Qur'an tell us to drive out the Jewish invaders?" they demanded.[4] They were unarmed, but angry. Mosab's father disagreed—he was a moderate, but he could not contradict the writings of the Qur'an. Eventually, in 1986, he and six other key Palestinian leaders formed Hamas to stir the Palestinians toward forming an independent state under Allah.

Mosab described this move of his father as climbing the "ladder" of Islam. The bottom rung of this ladder, he explains, is noble and attractive—prayer and praise to Allah. A few rungs higher you find activities like assisting the poor, setting up charities, providing schools. But at the top rung, but out of sight, lurks jihad, killing for the glory of god. Here you find the radicals. This is the danger of Islam. The moderates, he says, are the most dangerous, for you never know when they have taken the step to the top. His father would never have guessed where his first steps would lead, he reflected.

In 1987 a Palestinian uprising called the First Intifada began. Hamas took the lead, fuelling riots with stones and Molotov cocktails. Israelis responded fiercely and soon the cemeteries and hospitals were overflowing with victims. Because he was a Hamas leader, Mosab's father was arrested and tortured in an attempt to uncover the secrets of Hamas and break its power.

With the head of the house imprisoned for eighteen months, Mosab's family had no source of income. Friends who had previously flocked to their door now abandoned them, and the family was close to starving. Even his uncle attempted to shut down Mosab from selling cakes his mother cooked because his uncle was embarrassed by it. When the imprisonment was over, the "friends" flocked back again. Mosab was angry with this injustice and hypocrisy.

Hamas became more violent and aggressive. The Palestinians' cry was simple—Israelis were killing their children, the rest of the world was behind them, and Allah required it.

So the conflict escalated. Al Qassam emerged—an armed military wing of Hamas. Then when the Palestinians kidnapped and murdered an Israeli policeman, Israel responded with a massive crackdown, deporting 1,600 men, including Mosab's father. The world outcry led to the Oslo Accord, an agreement in which Yasser Arafat recognized the right for Israel to exist.

Then came the first suicide bomber, with car bombs and a massacre at Hebron. Mosab supported all this bloodshed. To him everything was black and white: "good" Palestinians and "bad" Israelis. His father wrestled with inner conflict; he could never be involved in the killings but could not oppose the teachings of the Qur'an that were used to justify the killing.

There were many Palestinian organizations devoted to destroying

Israel, but the two biggest were the PLO and Hamas. The PLO was a nationalist organization—political, not religious—and not all members were practising Muslims. It was committed to regaining all the territories owned prior to 1948 and gaining self-determination. Hamas, on the other hand, was a religious organization founded on the Qur'an. Both organizations hated the Israelis, but their ideologies were far apart. For the Israelis the PLO offered hope of negotiation, as it was political in nature. And progress was made with the Oslo accord in 1993, in which the PLO renounced the use of violence and acknowledged the right of Israel to exist, while Israel recognized the PLO as representative of the Palestinian people. Hamas, on the other hand, could never compromise on the land issue. The Qur'an told them the land was theirs and by the grace of Allah they would get it back. End of story.

So Hamas progressed into a full-blown terrorist organization, with many of its members on the top rung of the ladder of Islam. Moderates were powerless to resist the militants, who considered themselves backed by the full force of the Qur'an. On what basis could that be opposed?

Then in 1995 Israeli Prime Minister Rabin was murdered by a fanatical Jew. The world was on edge and put pressure on PLO leader Yasser Arafat to curb the power of Hamas. So the PLO rounded up all the leaders, including Mosab's father, together with thousands of Hamas members, locking them up in Palestinian prisons. Mosab was angry. He now hated the Palestinian Authority and Arafat, as well as Israel and secular Palestinians. He said, "Why should my father, who loved Allah and his people, have to pay such a heavy price while godless men like Arafat and his PLO handed a great victory to the Israelis—whom the Qur'an likened to pigs and monkeys?"[5]

Full of hate, and now approaching eighteen, Mosab purchased a gun and was arrested by the Israelis. As the son of a Hamas leader he was considered dangerous. Badly beaten, he was placed in a freezing room with a stinking vomit-soaked hood over his head. Chained to a low chair tilted forward, he was subjected to endless repetitive music so loud it made the chair vibrate. There was no letup, night or day. Other men he could not see cried, moaned, and screamed. One of them had been there three weeks and permitted only four hours of sleep a week. Three times a day Mosab was released for two minutes to eat his meal and use a toilet. During the day there were endless beatings and interrogations. At night the loud music and screams and moans of prisoners around him.

When the Shin Bet—the Israeli Intelligence service—eventually interviewed him, he decided to escape the interminable torture by agreeing become a spy. But his plan was to be a double agent and work against them. So he confessed to all he had done and agreed to cooperate under the code name Green Prince. So it was agreed. However he could not be released immediately or it would look suspicious to the Palestinians, so he had to serve out time in jail.

In prison he was shocked to discover that Hamas leaders in jail with him were torturing fellow prisoners suspected of collaborating with Israelis. As the son of Sheik Hussein Yousef, he was safe, he was treated like royalty; but the more vulnerable were not. Screams pierced the air daily. Mossab was given the task of copying the resultant "confessions" (because his writing was neat). He soon realized that most "confessions" were false—the tortured men only gave answers they were asked for—and their lives were ruined as a result. For the first time, he questioned his fundamental beliefs about Hamas and Islam, asking what was the difference between Israeli and Hamas torture, and who the real enemy was.

So when he was released from jail and had his first meeting with the Shin Bet, his radical views were somewhat moderated. Then to his surprise he found his handler (code named Laoi) showed respect for him and his culture, and instead of brainwashing him, taught principles that built him up. In fact, Laoi was more like his father than anyone he knew. He was confused. Then, surprisingly, his first mission was to attend college and get a degree financed by the Shin Bet. Gradually his hatred for them dissolved and he abandoned his plans to kill them.

Mosab told Laoi about the Hamas torture in the prisons, and asked why they didn't stop it. He gave two reasons: such a mentality was impossible to change and it helped destroy Hamas from the inside. Mosab's worldview took another blow.

Then one day Mosab and his friend Jamal were walking past

the Damascus gate in Jerusalem. This was the gate Paul of Tarsus would have used on his famous mission to destroy Christians, when God intercepted him and he became a believer. There, a Christian approached Mosab and invited him to a Christian gathering. Jamal later warned him it was dangerous, but Mosab was unfazed. His father had always taught Mosab to be open-minded. He owned a library of more than five thousand books, including a Bible. And Mosab was bored, and thought if Israelis like Laoi could teach him so much, maybe infidels could too. Besides, "after [being] with nominal Muslims, zealots, and atheists, the educated and the igno-rant, right-wingers and left-wingers, Jews and Gentiles, [he] wasn't picky anymore."[6]

Mosab loved the meeting and went home to read the New Testament he was given. He was blown away by Jesus and His Sermon on the Mount, and couldn't stop reading. He said, "Every verse seemed to touch a deep wound in my life."[7] Then Matthew 5:43–45 arrested him:

> You have heard that it was said, "Love your neighbor and hate your enemy." But I tell you, love your enemies and pray for those who persecute you, that you may be children of your Father in heaven.

He was "thunderstruck" by the passage. He had never heard any-thing like it and knew it was what he had been pursuing all his life.

For years he had struggled to identify his true enemy. Now he realized the enemy was not the Israelis or Hamas, or people who harmed him. It was the common enemy in each man and woman, things like greed and pride and evil. Five years before, he would have read these words and thought Jesus crazy. But his many painful experiences since then had joined forces to prepare him for the beauty of this truth.

Then he read Jesus' command, "Do not judge, or you too will be judged" (Matt. 7:1), and he thought of the gulf between Jesus and Allah. He observed that the god of Islam was very judgmental and Arab society mirrored that.

So he read on. Overwhelmed by the message, he began to cry.

He began to recognize God's hand in his life—first using the

Shin Bet to show him his enemy was not Israel, and then leading him to the New Testament to answer the rest of his quandaries.

But he still had a long way to go. The Muslims taught the Bible had been altered and was unreliable. And while he believed Jesus, he didn't equate Him with God.

He went to church and loved the reality of the faith of Christians he met there. They were not like other Christians he had known, whom he saw as no different from traditional Muslims, claiming a religion but not living it. He longed to bring the things he was learning to his people. He now saw that if their biggest desire was fulfilled—the return of their land—they would still be the same. There would still be bickering and fighting over trivialities. The land was not their problem; the problem lay within them.

With Hamas now crippled and its leaders imprisoned or divided, the second Palestinian uprising emerged (the Second Intifada) with terrible consequences. World media reported that the second intifada was a spontaneous protest from the people. Mosab, who witnessed its emergence from close quarters, instead put the blame squarely on the shoulders of a self-seeking Yasser Arafat, "a traitor who sold out his people for a ride on their shoulders"[8] using Mosab's father as a puppet to trigger the event. Rocks and Molotov cocktails quickly escalated to guns; Israel responded and tit for tat the violence escalated. Sickened by the deaths and injuries, and anxious to do what he could to reduce them, Mosab went back to the Shin Bet, giving it all he had.

Because of his close relationship with his father, a top Hamas leader, Mosab knew all that was going on. He was his father's "protégé, his bodyguard, his confidant, his student, and his friend."[9] So he became very effective. He was instrumental in discovering that Arafat's own bodyguards, funded by the USA and international donors, were involved in terrorism, and the evidence he uncovered was eventually used before the United Nations Security Council.

The intifada and bloodshed rolled on. Mosab was appalled and disgusted by the hypocrisy he saw on so many fronts. More and more he was being influenced by Jesus' teaching: forgive your enemies. He now began to compare his father with Jesus instead of the Qur'an. His father became less a hero, which broke Mosab's heart. His conscience was now becoming more sensitive, and when he uncovered terrorists he wrestled with the problem—what should be done with them? "Allah had no problem with murder," he said, "in fact, he insisted on it."[10] But now he had discovered Jesus, whose standards were higher, and he found he was no longer able to kill even terrorists.

A big test came when five would-be suicide bombers knocked on his door, asking for a place to stay. He set them up in an apartment and had it bugged. In deciding what should be their fate, his new ideologies won the day, and he persuaded the Shin Bet to imprison the terrorists instead of assassinating them.

His missions were now tremendously successful. Many deadly bombings were averted, many innocent lives saved. In his spare time he hung out with his Christian friends and drew strength from this link, becoming more and more conscious of the protecting hand of God on his life. One day he was driving home a notorious wanted terrorist when the terrorist's cell phone rang. It was Arafat's headquarters, warning that Israeli helicopters were following him. Mosab looked and saw them closing in. Then he heard God speak to his heart to turn left between two buildings. That put him momentarily out of sight from the helicopters. Then he heard God say, "Get out of the car and leave it." They jumped and ran, leaving the car with both doors open. The helicopter hovered briefly and left. Normally Laoi would have protected Mosab from such events, but this time he had been out of the operations room, and no one thought to ask if the car might belong to the Green Prince.

Eventually Mosab had so many successes he and Laoi were concerned he might be found out. They decided he had to be "sanitized." So the Shin Bet tricked the Israeli Defense Forces into believing Mosab was a terrorist so that they would arrest him, making Mosab "innocent" in the eyes of the Palestinians. When the IDF moved in for the arrest, Mosab escaped just a minute before. The media had been tipped off, and the result was Mosab became a Palestinian hero. All he had to do was keep clear of the IDF. But eventually the pressure of multiple role-playing wore him out and, with Laoi's approval, he allowed himself to be arrested so that he could serve his time in prison and emerge a true "hero" among the Palestinians.

But a strange thing happened. As he once again faced the captors who had tortured and abused him, he found not a trace of bitterness toward them. His only explanation was a verse in the Book of Hebrews (4:12):

> For the word of God is alive and active. Sharper than any double-edged sword, it penetrates even to dividing soul and spirit, joints and marrow; it judges the thoughts and attitudes of the heart.

He still didn't equate Jesus with God, but somehow the words of the Bible were pushing out his old hatred and replacing it with a love he didn't understand.

Then one day he received the knockout blow. A friend drew his attention to a TV program, a Coptic priest named Zakaria Botros.[2*] He was "performing an autopsy on the Qur'an,"[11] revealing faults and flaws of which Mosab had no previous knowledge. Resisting his angry instinct to switch it off, he began to see it as an answer to his prayers, and the discovery that Jesus is the Son of God. It severed his final links to Islam—an immensely difficult transition, like discovering your father is not really your father.

This event marked the completion of his six-year journey of becoming a Christian.

Eventually Mosab became discouraged. He was twenty-seven and asking questions. Who was he, what was his future, what girl could he marry, what could he talk to her about, what had he achieved, had the bloodshed stopped? So he told Laoi he was leaving. The Shin Bet strongly opposed it, but when Mosab broke contact for three months they ultimately agreed to help him escape to the USA, where he had Christian friends. Later, when Mosab's application for asylum was in danger of being rejected, Laoi learned about the

---

2 * Zakariah Botros has been on air with his teaching since 2003. It is estimated that fifty million Muslims hear him daily, many becoming Christians as a result. Pointing out flaws in the Muslim faith and teaching Muslims how Jesus can meet their needs, he is considered Islam's greatest foe. He lives in hiding, a reported $60 million dollar bounty on his head. (By comparison Osama bin Laden attracted a bounty of "only" $25 million!)

crisis. Now retired from the Shin Bet, he contacted Mosab and came to America—at great personal expense—to support the application.

When Mosab's family learned he had become a Christian they were devastated. His father was inconsolable and "cried like a baby," believing Mosab had destroyed his future and the future of his family, and one day Mosab would be "taken to hell before his eyes, and then we will be estranged forever."[12] When Mosab's book was published and became a best seller, Mosab grieved over the loss of his family and the impact it would have on them. "Who will marry my sisters?" he lamented. His father formally and publicly disowned him.

Mosab now works to spread the knowledge of Jesus, particularly to Muslims. He is modest in his faith, acknowledging his need to grow and his dependence on God, of whom he says, "I feel Him. I love His work. God is not a drug in my life…He is my inspiration, my leader, my teacher my guide."[13] He says while he is not religious, when he goes to church it is not to socialize but to worship.

He concludes:

> I was a devout follower of a religion that required strict adherence to rigid regulations in order to please the god of the Qur'an and get into heaven.
>
> I had money, power, and position in my former life, but what I wanted was freedom. And that meant, among other things, leaving behind hate, prejudice, and a desire for revenge.
>
> The message of Jesus—love your enemies—is what finally set me free. It no longer mattered who my friends were or who my enemies were; I was supposed to love them all. And I could have a loving relationship with a God who would help me love others.[14]

So What Is Happening?

Muslims becoming Christians—the stories abound. Just google "Muslims become Christians" and you find multiple websites filled with testimonies from around the world. Many have experienced God in powerful and different ways. With the spotlight on Islam over the last decade, it is worth making a few observations about what is happening.

One valuable source is a compilation of papers: *From the Straight Path to the Narrow Way,* compiled by David Greenlee. The papers were the work of twenty missionaries, missiologists, and practitioners actively involved with Muslims.

A major issue they examine is why Muslims choose to leave their faith and follow Christ. The reasons have to be compelling, because in almost every case conversion to Christianity results in severe persecution for the convert. Islam is more than a religion— it penetrates every aspect of life—especially family. If someone departs from the faith, their family members suffer severe shame amongst their community. So they invariably pressure the convert to renounce his or her new beliefs, with anything from hostile words to threats of murder. One convert lamented, "The tears of my mother were harder to bear than the beatings from my father."[15] A small study in Pakistan showed that women suffered the worst— out of seven women who converted, three were murdered, whereas out of sixty men, only one was murdered.[16] So when this is the price people are willing to pay, we ask what it is that attracts them.

One study noted three major influences:

- Muslim converts had seen and experienced sacrificial love shown by Christians

- They had read some portions of Scripture (passage most mentioned was the Sermon on the Mount—Matthew 5—which has its emphasis on humility and forgiveness)

- They had experienced a special manifestation of the power of Christ

Another fascinating and unexpected influence was dreams and visions. One of the papers (by Dr. J. Dudley Woodberry from Fuller Theological Seminary) studied 650 former Muslims from 40 countries and 58 ethnic groups. The study found a remarkable 27 percent of converts were influenced by dreams and visions.[17] A further study in Central Asia noted that 15 percent experienced dreams about God in the conversion process.[18]

The visions were varied. Often the image described was Jesus—typically radiating light or wearing white. An Algerian woman had a vision of her Muslim grandmother coming into her room and saying, "Jesus is not dead; He is here." In Israel an Arab dreamed that his deceased father said, "Follow the pastor. He will show you the right way."[19] A man from Saudi Arabia wrote: "One night I had this horrible dream of me being taken into hell....Suddenly one day, Jesus appeared to me and said, 'Son, I am the way, the truth, and the life. And if you would...follow Me, I would save you from the hell that you have seen'...So I started looking for a Christian who could give me advice about this Jesus I have seen and possibly get one of the Christian Holy Books, which I now know is the Bible."[20]

A different kind of study by Andreas Maurer provided illuminating insights by comparing ten converts from Islam to Christianity with ten who converted the other way—from Christianity to Islam.

The ten who became Christians were mainly influenced by love shown through Christ in the Bible and warmth among Christians. Another factor was the hope and assurance found in Christianity and a joyful, vital relationship with Jesus. South Africans found all this lacking in Islam, with its rituals and incomprehensible Arabic expressions.

The ten who converted the other way—from Christianity to Islam—considered Christianity to be impractical and "against common reason." Doctrines such as the Trinity and Christ's incarnation were stumbling blocks. By contrast, the converts found Islam more consistent with science and the enlightened mind.

Maurer said:

> It is significant that six out of ten converts to Christianity said that a supernatural experience contributed greatly to their decision to convert, whereas none of the ten converts to Islam mentioned this motive...The converts appeared to be convinced that God had spoken to them in a direct way.[21]

Another paper by missionary Abraham Duran, serving a non-Arab people in the Middle East and Central Asia, had these comments on the effect of the supernatural on Muslims:

Remarkable answers to prayer brought the reality of the kingdom of heaven before the eyes of their [Muslim] friends— sometimes as dreams, visions, healings, and prophecy. Not everyone who experienced the reality of the kingdom in this way became believers. Some even today would ask team members to pray for them when they are sick but would not give their lives to Jesus.[22]

Another factor listed by converts to Christianity was thirst for truth/certainty. While Islam has a reputation as a religion of reason and truth, present-day Islam is torn by quarrels and violence. Conflicting interpretations of their religion divide Muslims amongst themselves, and as a result some look elsewhere to find answers.

Forgiveness and redemption were also key factors in bringing Muslims to Christ. Islam stresses the importance of righteous living and warns that sin can lead to hell, but it offers no certainty of forgiveness. By contrast, Christianity presents a Savior who took our sin on Himself, and offers free pardon to all who change their ways and receive it by faith. This was an important aspect for many converts.

So Hindus and Muslims, and people from all other faiths, are finding what they are seeking in the person of Jesus Christ. They are finding everything that is good and holy, and the end of their journey is wrapped up in this remarkable person. But is Christianity all good?

Chapter 24
CHRISTIAN EVIL
By Dr. Ken Chant

W HAT DO WE make of the times when Christians are responsible for evil? What of the Inquisition, the Crusades, the witch burnings? We asked Dr. Ken Chant this question. He wrote this in response:

Christians have murdered people, raped and robbed them, burnt them to death, tortured and enslaved them, and committed a multitude of other barbarities, all in the name of Christ. Some thought they were pleasing God by their actions. Others, ruled by greed, lust for power, love of violence, craving empire, callously used the church to further their own foul goals.

But much the same can be said of all major religions—Islam has countless victims, and Buddhism, Hinduism, and others, are far from guiltless.

Does this make religion wrong? Hardly, for the secular world is even more guilty of mass slaughter—think about Napoleon, Hitler, Stalin, Pol Pot, and their ilk, both ancient and modern. Secularism, humanism, communism, atheism, have behaved with worse butchery of millions than the Church ever did.

What then can we say about violent behavior by Christians? Simply that the Church is made of people, all sorts of people, most of them genuinely good, but with enough of the other kind to be a source of occasional mayhem. Yet across the centuries for every church leader who has abused his position, there have been thousands of humble, ordinary priests, pastors, clergy who have faithfully and lovingly tended their flocks across long and fruitful lives. If that had not been the case, the Church would soon have lost the allegiance of its people and would have been trashed.

Indeed, no one who is truly Christian, and rightly following

Christ, would ever resort to violence to gain a convert or to reap some personal advantage.

History shows that it is usually perilous for the Church to become numerically dominant, or to gain too much wealth and power. Whenever that state is reached, the Church becomes appealing to unscrupulous people, who find ways to infiltrate it and corrupt its godly purpose. But every time that has happened, many true Christians have broken away and started a smaller, purer, godly Church, radiant with the love of Christ. Or instead, within the decadent Church, prophetic voices have spoken out (Luther, Calvin, Wesley, and so on) to call it back to its proper character and mission.

In the meantime, it is worth asking how many hospitals, orphanages, schools, welfare groups, refuges, counseling centers the atheists of the world have built.

The medieval Crusades against Islam are sometimes cited as proof of the innate evil of Christianity. But of course, even a loose knowledge of history will show that religion was not the true reason but only an excuse for the Crusades. Giving the warring barons and kings of dark Europe someone to fight, other than each other, was a strong motivation. Conquest and plunder were another. There were also elements of base fanaticism, social envy, cultural ignorance, and, frequently, just the sheer love of fighting by illiterate leaders who had all their lives been trained to do nothing else.

The Inquisition is also cited as proof that religion is a menace to civilised life. Even Roman Catholics are embarrassed by the horrors that their inquisitors imposed upon thousands of helpless victims. Likewise in witch-burnings, drawing and quartering of Catholic priests, and other barbarities, Protestants in the past moved far away from Christian love. There was scant difference between Protestant savagery and the kind practiced by Rome.

Can such wickedness be excused, justified, or even explained? Not really. No one today fully understands, for example, the spasm of witch-burning that overtook Europe for two or three centuries. It rose quickly, and in the end died away just as quickly. The reasons for such aberrations, including the Inquisition, are complex, hard to penetrate, and had much more to do with the social, cultural, political, and commercial climate of those times than with religion. If religion had been the primary cause, then such abuse by the church of ordinary people would have been a constant part of church history, which of course it was not.

But even if in the entire world only corrupt Christians could be found, that would still not make Christianity wrong. The truth or falsehood of the gospel has to be determined by factual evidence, not by ad hominem (personal) arguments. Let us ignore personal considerations and rest our case upon reason. Even what I said above about atheists is actually not a good argument. Only word-poor disputants depend upon accusing each other rather than contesting the beliefs they represent.

Plainly, no matter how wonderful the dogma, nor how true it may be, wherever you find people you will find faults! To err is human. So there are good and bad people wherever one looks, which proves nothing except itself. So I would say to those [who] would denounce the gospel, forget about the bad things, and even the good things that the church is said to have done. The gospel of Christ stands or falls upon the Man who preached it, and who died and rose again to make its truth indestructible forever.[1]

Dr. Chant is president of Vision Christian College (Australia) with about 120,000 students around the world. He has spent many years as an active pastor, and has been the principal of four Bible colleges.

The stories you have read so far are remarkable and dramatic. But not everyone has a story that is remarkable and dramatic. What are the rest like; the "ordinary" people? The final section opens with brief stories that were posted on a website as a response to the challenge of the Global Atheist Convention held in Melbourne in 2012.

SECTION 6: WIND-UP

Chapter 25
MY STORIES

MICHELLE HARLEY

At seventeen I walked away from my Anglican upbringing and sought happiness in my own wants and desires. Married at twenty, divorced by twenty-eight, I continued seeking happiness and fulfillment in all the wrong places. After thirteen years of conflict with my ex-husband, problems with my children, tensions in my second marriage, the death of my ex-husband (and much more) I needed something solid to build my life on. In 2005 I encountered the one true God in the person of Jesus Christ. I found His love to be the rock that I could build my life on and I now know true happiness is to trust in Him.

SHERYL MINNS

All my life I was subjected to constant criticism, judgment, and condemnation from my family and the world. I was never allowed to forget how flawed and fallen I was, and never forgiven for it. So I grew up chronically depressed, with no desire to strive or achieve because I believed no matter what I did, I would never please anyone.

Then I discovered that in spite of my serious imperfection, God loved me so much that He took the penalty for all my sins, all my flaws, and all my failings. Imagine what a relief it was to find that I was acceptable to God, simply because Jesus had already paid for my faults! Now I understand that I don't have to be perfect, because I'm already forgiven.

LAUREN DEVENISH

I have hope in God. Not an "I'd like it to happen" hope, but a rock-solid, time-tested certainty that He is real. That He is good. That He is powerful. That He has a plan and a purpose for this world and for me, and that He loves me more than I'll ever comprehend. I have no outstanding miracles to tell, but the everyday hope of a faithful God who never lets me down. He is real!

Amy Joy

I'm thirty-one now and was an atheist for over twenty years. But eleven months ago, through some Christians showing me unconditional love, I was healed from a number of physical issues, healed from depression and anxiety and freed from drug addiction. The best part was that, because I had tried so hard on my own strength to overcome these issues and failed every time, when I was healed I KNEW it was Jesus who had done it and not me. So I now give my whole life to Him. Glory to Jesus!

David von Blanckensee

I had regular migraines for ten years. A friend prayed with me and I was healed. I have not had any migraines since. It's now been more than ten years! I love when God does stuff like this.

Catherine Pavone

It was about three and a half years ago that things changed profoundly for me when I asked Jesus into my heart. Before then I felt I was just "existing," and I felt ashamed and help-less about the direction my life had taken. My local maternal health nurse referred me to MOPS (a local Mothers of Preschoolers playgroup) that was held in a nearby church. The genuine friendships I made there and the philosophy "mothers can change the world" steered my life along an amazing path. Some of the mothers in the group introduced me to a wonderful local church and as a result I decided to make God the center of my life again.

For the first time in ten years, I felt a sense of peace and that I belonged somewhere. I felt that I could unload my past burdens and start afresh. My heart was filled to the brim with this amazing hope and love from God. I felt God saw me as a precious child of His and that His love for me is as deep as the oceans and as magnificent as a soaring eagle. I saw my life as having a sense of purpose and that God would guide me along the right path. He is my compass and I no longer need to be afraid as I have the living presence of God within me.

BRYAN GRASBY

I went to a church nearly thirty-three years ago for all the wrong reasons, I didn't like the singing, I didn't like the message and I didn't respond to the preacher's call to become a Christian. But then I heard an audible voice telling me "this is your last chance." I went to the front, repented of my many sins and accepted Christ as my Lord and Savior. I felt my sins lift of me like a damp blanket right there on the spot! Jesus came into my life that day; He changed me (and in time my circumstances) and has set me on a path for His glory! So many amazing things and wonderful opportunities have come my way since that day! I thank You, Jesus, for all You have done for me, and are still doing for me, and will continue to do for me, as I live for You!

EMMA FABER

My first miraculous encounter with God was when, at the age of fifteen, I attempted to commit suicide by standing in front of an oncoming train. For about four years I had been unable to cry or look at myself in a mirror without severely hating what I saw. The lens I saw myself through was completely distorted. To end the emotional pain I wanted to end my life, and after two failed attempts, I calmly stood in front of a rapidly approaching train, locked my feet just inside the rails, closed my eyes and waited...Time seemed to slow down, I felt a rush of warm wind blow past my head, I opened my eyes and was stunned to find myself about six meters away from the tracks. Now, I know that I *did not move* but something physically moved me!

Three months later I had an equally miraculous encounter

with Jesus (the God that I previously didn't believe in!) when He literally lifted the tremendous weight of years of self-hate and emotional blockages off my shoulders and I felt free for the first time in my life. Now, twenty years and many genuine life-altering miracles later, I still feel His presence beside me at all times, and hear His unmistakably gentle voice speaking daily and deeply into my heart... now that's real!

HELEN CLIFFE

My God is amazing. I was healed of hay fever after I was prayed for by my friends. I trusted in God and He healed me. How good is that!

ANTHONY FERNANDO

Growing up in a Christian family I knew about God, and about what Jesus had done for us, but that's all it was...knowledge. I fell away from God through my high school years and started walking down a pathway of rebellion and destruction and violence. My brother died of a heroin overdose when I was seventeen, which really warped my outlook to life. I thought to myself that we were only born to die, so I valued my life very little.

Over the next eight years I became addicted to a variety of drugs. I would abuse my body every weekend with speed, ecstasy, and, when really pushing for a rush, substances like amyl nitrate and ice. I eventually became a drug courier, and then trafficked full time for about two and a half years. The worst of my drug addictions was my love of smoking weed. No matter what I tried, I could never stop. I travelled overseas several times to try and dry out a bit, but picked up where I left off when I got back. I was like a puppet, with drugs holding the strings. I needed to smoke in order to eat, sleep, and even wake up—if that makes sense! (The 4:00 a.m. pipes.) My life was going nowhere fast.

I began to realize I was in trouble and there was nothing I could do about it—on my own, anyway. This whole time I was living a complete double life. None of my family had any idea what my life was like; I hid it so well.

One day I was thinking about it and running one get-clean strategy after another through my mind. Suddenly I felt something inside tell me to confide in someone who didn't know about where I was at. I chose my mother. At first she didn't believe me. I mean, in her eyes, her son was just a good son—I never brought any problems home.

When she realized the seriousness of the situation, she locked in and invited me to church. I don't remember what the sermon was about that day. All I know was that something was calling to my heart go up to the front of the church and receive prayer.

As I stood there reaching out to God for help I was encountered by His amazing undeniable presence. Suddenly everything I knew about Jesus became real for me! I understood forgiveness like I never had before; guilt, shame, and torment just dropped off me like shackles. I felt my spirit come alive—although for those first few weeks I felt so tired that I would repeatedly have visions of Jesus carrying me from a torture cell. The Holy Spirit breathed life into me, and I felt so free! Everything was different now, I felt free to be the Anthony that I was born to be; I didn't have to put up a bold front or persona to protect myself anymore. Everyone commented on how my appearance suddenly changed. I was constantly told I was glowing.

I never touched any drugs ever again since then—it's been just over three years now. By the grace of God and His enabling power and strength, I stopped smoking cigarettes within about three weeks. All this was only the start of how God has transformed my life, but over the last three years He has done SO much more.

KAY PAINTER

I believed the "it's just tissue" story, and it was "not in my plans." But when I saw the little body, as they threw it in the trash, my selfishness crumbled. It would be two failed suicides and years of more bad choices and guilt until I found Jesus Christ. Like others I believed abortion was good for women. Firsthand I can tell you it is not so. Through Christ I have found forgiveness and peace, the kind you can't deny or make up. If you could see me now and then, you too would realize He lives! He is real.

Peter Stevens

When I was in my early thirties I felt I had everything. Good job, house paid off, beautiful wife, and four beautiful children. One problem: my wife went all "spiritual" on me. She started talking about Jesus and going to all these weird meetings. Then her new friends started meeting in our home! It was crazy. And they let me know they were praying for me! That made me mad. I remember the first time they got me to church I was quite drunk and it was all very hazy and strange.

Eventually, after four years I was at the point of leaving or doing something to end all the harassment. They had been telling me all I had to do was "accept Jesus" and ask Him into my heart.

Anyway, to cut a long story short, I decided to give it a go— at least then I would know they were wrong, and I could get on with my life! But, I said the words, and unexpectedly, I found out that He (Jesus) did come in when I invited Him. I totally changed, and have been getting to know Him more and more every day since (I am now fifty-nine). It has been really, really great! I love Jesus and would never want to leave Him.

Marlene Smith

My father was a Muslim and I was a secret believer (in Jesus) till I took the bold step to be baptized at eighteen years of age. Now in my old age I can testify to His never-failing love, not only for me but for the whole world.

All these people found God though they have never seen Him. Why is God out of sight? Why doesn't He show up, remove all doubt, and show us how we should run our lives? Wouldn't that be a better way? Here is the answer to that common question.

Chapter 26
WHEN TEACHER STEPPED OUT

OUR NOSES WERE down at our desks as we labored at the project the teacher had set, so we didn't notice when he left the room. He hadn't said he was going and he had never left us like that before, so when it dawned on us, we were mystified. As the minutes ticked by, we became more intrigued and more aware that the cat was away. Some of the mischief-makers began to stir.

Like every school, we had our share of fads that came and went. Sometimes marbles, sometimes swap cards, sometimes football, sometimes stink bombs or water bombs. It could be anything. This time it was shooting folded paper pellets with a rubber band. The craze was at its peak, and a golden opportunity had been gifted to us.

It wasn't the "bad boy" of the class who began it that day. It was a teacher's pet who was always careful not to get caught. A cunning player, he consistently managed to fly under teacher's radar. So when no one was watching he launched the first pellet at the class bad boy, then jammed his nose back into his book. The bad boy, not realizing who was responsible, drew his own weapon and fired at a suspect. That boy entered the fray and so it escalated. In no time the air was thick with flying missiles. A few students abandoned their seats to war from behind benches or desks, as laughter and cries of pain mingled with the general bedlam.

So it escalated, but not everyone was involved. In the midst of the mayhem, several students continued working. The only thing different was their body position—lower—to evade flying pellets. In that way they plugged away at their tasks, faithful to teacher's wishes.

The battle raged, most of us blissfully unaware of the escalating noise and mayhem. A teacherless classroom was heaven and we made the most of it. Then, at the peak of the chaos, a shadow fell across the room. In a millisecond—which seemed like an eternity—the truth dawned. It could not have been worse. Filling the doorway was the hulking figure of Charlie Rivers, the biggest and most feared teacher in the school. Our hearts sank. But the fact was, no one had ever actually witnessed him in action. His visual presence had always been enough to tame the worst troublemaker. But our imaginations ran wild as we took in those massive arms, the elephant-like neck, and the barrel chest. In those days corporal punishment was standard fare, and we were caught red-handed. This was awful trouble. To make a long story short, Charlie cleaned up big time. Meticulously searching every pocket of every student, he collected a pile of pellets and dozens of rubber bands in a chalk box, and dealt with the offenders. He purged the class of all elements of our crime, and that was the end of shooting pellets with rubber bands.

The whole process probably took no more than twenty minutes, but I learned something. I learned just how quickly the character of every student could be brought to light by the simple act of teacher leaving the room. If that classroom had been covered by CCTV cameras, a simple analysis of the footage could have ranked every student's behavior from worst to best—and with some surprises. The class "bad boy," for example, was not the first to stir trouble; it was the *closet* bad boy, flushed out by the simple process of teacher leaving the room.

I imagine this is why God has "left the room." Why He has placed Himself out of sight; why some people can kid themselves God does not exist. God is simply testing what is in hearts. Life on Earth is, above all, a test. It is a test designed to separate sheep from goats, so that God can reward those who have followed Him and His ways, embrace them into His family, enjoy a relationship with them, and ultimately bring them to His holy heaven forever. This is how He finds who they are.

Whenever Charlie Rivers was in sight, we were angels, at our best behavior. Similarly, if we knew God lurked behind our shoulder, we would live as innocent lambs. Who would transgress with God breathing down your neck? But that scenario doesn't work for God. It compromises freedom, freedom to be ourselves. And God will not do that. Freedom is not negotiable. God wants sons and daughters, not slaves. He wants people who choose to give Him their love freely and joyfully, just as He freely gave His love to us.

So we live in a world where Teacher has "stepped out," where people can convince themselves God does not know, a world where we have true freedom to make the choice to love God and live in His holy ways, or to live for self and indulge the whims of sin and selfishness.

And we see all kinds of responses to that freedom. We see in our world a potpourri of God's offspring who have chosen lives of agnosticism, faithful humble belief, self-centeredness, bitter unbelief, atheism, church-going agnosticism, good citizenship without God, complacency, ignorance, education, narcissism, planet-saving, or social work, etc.

God loves all these with an infinite love, but His only intrusion in their lives is a still, small voice that from time to time whispers, "this is the way, walk in it." After which He silently steps aside, testing the heart.

Of course, there is a day of reckoning. Our classroom rebellion met its end when Charlie Rivers unpacked his authority and power. So too will the sinner's rebellion meet its end when he goes to his Maker. The Bible doesn't overemphasize the judgment part of God's nature—his mercy triumphs over judgment—but it is definitely there. It should be a motivator, along with a natural response to the love God shows us.

So how have you responded to God's still, small voice? And if you have never engaged with God, do you know how to go about it? The process is not complicated. Here are a couple of simple steps.

The first has to do with holiness. God is holy—holy beyond our imagination. And He does not tolerate violations to that holiness. That is bad news for us, for we are unholy. All of us have a bent toward sin.

Our sin disqualifies us from engaging with God. The good news is that God has made a way to get over that problem. It involves firstly recognition of our sin and taking responsibility for it, followed by a change in attitude toward it—called repentance, changing our ways. Repentance is an attitude more than anything else, an attitude that lines up with God's attitude to sin. (He hates it!) Of course, repentance has an outworking. When faced with temptation to sin, we put out our hands and push it away to the utmost of our ability.

For people who choose that path, God steps in with the rest. He forgives willingly. His forgiveness is rooted in the work of Jesus in His death on the cross. Jesus was punished in our place—the ultimate expression of love for us—so that we could be free of the consequences of our sin.

That forgiveness is a free gift, and we embrace it by a simple faith act—a grateful prayer, "God we accept this gift," and a simple belief that we now own it.

Not only does that bring us forgiveness, it supernaturally brings the Spirit of God into our hearts. The impact of that is profound— God living inside us!

The realization of God's love in all this stimulates a life devoted to God and His people and His church. It opens the door to a life of divine interventions such as those you have read in this book. If you have never joined your life to God, now is the best time. Make the step, embrace God, learn about Jesus in the New Testament, and find a Bible-believing church. Enjoy your newfound heavenly Father and help spread the good news you have discovered.

(If you don't have a Bible, google "Bible Gateway.")

The Tests of God

Remember how the LORD your God led you all the way in the wilderness these forty years, to humble and test you in order to know what was in your heart, whether or not you would keep his commands.

—DEUTERONOMY 8:2

The LORD your God is testing you to find out whether you love him with all your heart and with all your soul.

—DEUTERONOMY 13:3

Though you probe my heart, though you examine me at night and test me, you will find that I have planned no evil; my mouth has not transgressed.

—PSALM 17:3

The crucible for silver and the furnace for gold, but the LORD
tests the heart.

—PROVERBS 17:3

Those on the rocky ground are the ones who receive the word
with joy when they hear it, but they have no root. They believe
for a while, but in the time of testing they fall away.

—LUKE 8:13

[Jesus] asked this only to test [Phillip], for he already had in
mind what he was going to do.

—JOHN 6:6

We are not trying to please people but God, who tests our
hearts.

—1 THESSALONIANS 2:4

Dear friends, do not be surprised at the fiery ordeal that has
come on you to test you, as though something strange were
happening to you.

—1 PETER 4:12

Since you have kept my command to endure patiently, I will
also keep you from the hour of trial that is going to come on
the whole world to test the inhabitants of the earth.

—REVELATION 3:10

Chapter 27
OUTRO

CHRISTIANS DON'T HAVE just philosophical knowledge of God, they have access to a dynamic spiritual experience, and millions tell of countless interventions in their lives as they walked with God."

I wrote these words in the introduction, and in the chapters that followed you read about a number of divine interventions and God discoveries. Reflect on a few of them for a moment:

The Atheist Philosopher: "In a giant turnaround, he methodically abandoned all his ideas, confessing all in his book *There Is a God*."

The Miracle: "After the prayer she asked for her leg plasters to be removed, and she stood up and walked."

The Honest Atheist: "Something changed in the faces of the [African Christians] we passed and spoke to: something in their eyes, the way they approached you direct, man-to-man, without looking down or away."

The Guilt-Ridden Crim: "The stars cannot tell, the moon cannot say, the change in me since Jesus came into my life."

The Marxist Atheist: "I fell flat on my back. I cried for an hour. I had an encounter with God."

The Scientists:

- Dr. Richard Smalley: "He learned that he did not need to throw his mind away when reading the Bible."

- Dr. Matti Leisola: "Those believing in a naturalistic explanation for the origin of life are the ones with a blind faith."

- Dr. Stuart Burgess: "The difficulty of designing and building things that are relatively simple makes you realize how great is the wisdom and power of God who has made all things."

The Songwriter: "[God] is going to give you…a song that will be easily sung by masses of people…easily translated into other languages."

The Intellectually Disabled Son: "The angel put the words on my head and told me to write it down."

The Rebellious Son: "I felt His presence in a way I could never deny. This was not brainwashing. This was truth. This was power. Suddenly I was sobbing, crying out to God with every fiber of my soul."

The Hindu Guru: "Tons of darkness seemed to lift and a brilliant light flooded my soul."

The Muslim: "He was blown away by Jesus and His Sermon on the Mount, and couldn't stop reading. He said, 'Every verse seemed to touch a deep wound in my life.'"

"A remarkable 27 percent of converts were influenced by dreams and visions."

The Gaming Addict: "Jesus has completely broken my addiction. My desire for gaming has gone.

My Stories: "I no longer need to be afraid as I have the living presence of God with me"…"I heard an audible voice telling me 'this is your last chance'"…"He literally lifted the tremendous weight of years of self-hate and emotional blockages off my shoulders"…"I was constantly told I was glowing"

These stories are living, dynamic testimonials to the reality of God, thorns in the atheist's side. If they were scarce, if we could only scratch up one or two flimsy stories, the atheist could sleep at night, confident his case was secure. But the stories are not scarce and they are not flimsy; they are abundant and robust.

Each testimony eminently reinforces what we already know in our hearts—God is real and God is good. Those who remain unconvinced typically sit where scientist Dr. Matt Leisola once sat: "*Without realizing it, I was a typical product of the western naturalistic educational system and I certainly wanted to remain autonomous, and actually hated the idea of God interfering with my life.*" A mind-set like that is a prison to truth. But an honest reappraisal opened this scientist's eyes to the real world, and he found God.

I pray the evidence of this book may persuade you to look again and find what is there to be found. And if you are a believer, I pray these stories have strengthened your faith for the work God does through you.

Is there more to learn about finding God? Much more. It can fill libraries. As a new Christian you will learn much of it by attending a dynamic church. While you are finding one of those, there is a subject that cropped up in several of the stories and was crucial to the outcome. It is the baptism in the Holy Spirit. This is a *must*. It needs explanation, so here it is.

Chapter 28
THE POWER SOURCE

My Story

AFTER FINDING GOD, I then discovered some intriguing verses about the Holy Spirit—and speaking in tongues. I asked a Christian about the Holy Spirit and speaking in tongues, but he didn't know much about it. I was troubled. It seemed I was missing something. So I asked God could I please have this Holy Spirit "thing." No complaints and no problems if I was mistaken, but if I was missing out, please grant my prayer.

Some time later I went to a Saturday night Christian youth meeting and sat way down the back. I was still finding my way, and a little wary of other Christians. With a back seat close to the exit, I felt "safe." They were singing some happy songs and hymns, and suddenly, for no obvious reason, I felt God's presence come on me. A warm glow filled me and steadily magnified its intensity, eventually becoming so overpowering I thought I would fall over. It was like liquid ecstasy. I knew it was God—the Holy Spirit—and I asked Him to stop, I was so concerned about falling over and making a big scene. I had to make a supreme effort to walk out when the meeting ended. No one else seemed to be in the least way affected as I was. As I drove home, I was overwhelmed with a love for the whole world. I felt like shouting strange words—realizing later I was on the verge of speaking in tongues. The feeling slowly faded over the next five days.

Several years later I learned more about the experience of the baptism of the Holy Spirit and speaking in tongues. After prayer, I received the ability to speak in tongues and learned how to make it work in my life. This had a profound effect on me—God became more real, the Bible more alive. Ever since then it has been a crucial part of my everyday life.

It was late December in the year 1900; the dawn of the twentieth century. Charles Parham, the leader of a small Bible school in Los Angeles, had given his students an unusual task. The Bible promised Christian believers a miraculous experience called the baptism in the Holy Spirit. "How," he asked them, "can we know we have received it? Is there some indicator or sign that accompanies the experience?"

The students set about searching their Bibles and finally came up with the answer. On the basis of the biblical evidence, they concluded that speaking in tongues was the sign that accompanied the baptism of the Holy Spirit.

So they began praying for the Holy Spirit. To their amazement, one of the girls began speaking in tongues. Soon others had the same experience and, in the ensuing months and for several years, there followed what became known as the Azusa Street revival, which sparked fires around the world. Many thousands received this new and strange experience. Lives were transformed, faith was ignited, and the supernatural gifts of the Holy Spirit were witnessed. (See 1 Corinthians 12:8.)

However, many other Christians considered the experience a heresy and ostracized the new movement. So they established their own denomination, which became known as the Pentecostal church.

These Pentecostals remained largely isolated until the sixties, when an American Episcopalian (Anglican) minister received the Holy Spirit and spoke in tongues. This man managed to weather the storms that followed and remain in his church. Thousands followed his example, in all mainstream denominations. Many Catholics were affected. It became known as the Charismatic movement.

The lives of these Pentecostals and Charismatics were also marked by other supernatural gifts (healing, miracles, prophecy, etc.) and strong spiritual zeal.

The baptism in the Holy Spirit and speaking in tongues was a normal part of the early New Testament church, as we will see. It gradually disappeared as the church declined in faith, though outpourings were recorded down through the centuries. For example, it is mentioned in the writings of Irenaeus (AD 150), Tertullian (AD 200), and Pachomius (AD 300). It was recorded that Francis Xavier spoke in tongues (AD 1552), also the Huguenots (AD 1685), the early Quakers (AD 1700), Wesleyans (AD 1750), and many others.

At the end of the twentieth century and the beginning of the third millennium, the Pentecostal and Charismatic movements have made a huge impact on Christianity around the world. It is without doubt a modern day Christian phenomenon.

What are the facts about the experience? The Bible tells us all we need to know. The common questions asked are:

- What is the purpose of the baptism in the Holy Spirit?
- Is it a separate experience from salvation?
- Does speaking in tongues always accompany the experience?
- Is the experience for all Christians?
- How do we receive this gift?

THE PURPOSE

In Acts 1:8, Jesus said, "You will receive power when the Holy Spirit comes on you; and you will be my witnesses." This experience is not for forgiveness of sins—it is to equip believers for service—particularly for spreading the good news that Jesus has died for our sins.

Consider Jesus' example. For thirty years, He was an unknown carpenter. Then the Holy Spirit came upon Him, and immediately His amazing miracles and compelling preaching made Him the talking point of the nation. (See Luke 3:21–22; 4:14.)

So, too, the disciples' ministry began in power when the Holy Spirit was poured out on them (Acts 2).

The experience is real, tangible, and effective in making us fruitful servants of God. The Holy Spirit baptism gives us power to witness and serve.

A SEPARATE EXPERIENCE

The baptism in the Holy Spirit is not the same as salvation (being born of the Holy Spirit). Being born of the Holy Spirit (salvation) gives entry to the kingdom of God, whereas the Holy Spirit baptism gives the believer power for service. Clear distinction between salvation and the baptism in the Holy Spirit is found in the following passages:

- In Acts 8:2–17, Philip preached to the Samaritans, who believed the good news of Jesus and were baptized. Remembering that "he who believes and is baptized will be saved" (Mark 16:16, NKJV), we can be certain these Samaritans were saved. Yet, the Holy Spirit (baptism) had not come down on them. This happened several days later when Peter and John made the trip down from Jerusalem and prayed for them.

- In Acts 19:2, Paul asked the Ephesians, "Did you receive the Holy Spirit when you believed?" His question implied a distinction between the two experiences. In other words, it is possible to be a believer and not to have received the Holy Spirit baptism.

- In John 4:14 and 7:37–39, Jesus compared salvation (eternal life) to a well of water, but He compared the Holy Spirit to rivers of living water, flowing out from the believer.

So the Holy Spirit is a dramatic experience that follows salvation, equipping us to serve God effectively.

Does Speaking in Tongues Always Accompany the Experience?

To answer this we check what happened in the Bible when the Holy Spirit was first poured out. Remember that Jesus is the One who baptizes us in the Holy Spirit (John 1:33), and He does not change (Heb. 13:8), so we can expect the same things to happen today. Here is what happened back then:

Acts 2: Pentecost

On this Day of Pentecost, the Holy Spirit fell—with the sound of a mighty wind, tongues of fire, and people speaking in tongues. The effect on people was so dramatic that observers accused them of drunkenness.

Acts 8:17–18: Samaria

No specific manifestations are recorded here. However, the Holy Spirit's impact was so tangible that the infamous magician Simon offered money to buy this power. He had been amazed by remarkable healings and other miracles, but it was the Holy Spirit gift that drew him most. We can only assume that the Holy Spirit manifestations Simon witnessed were the same as those in the other outpourings in Acts.

Acts 10:44–48: The Gentiles

These Gentiles (non-Jews) spoke in tongues and praised God when the Holy Spirit fell on them.

Note that Peter, describing this event later, said, "The Holy Spirit came on them as he had come on us at the beginning" (Acts 11:15). Their experiences were identical, but speaking in tongues was the only common manifestation.

Acts 19:1–6: Ephesus

These disciples spoke in tongues and prophesied when they received the Holy Spirit.

In summary

Several manifestations are described in these passages: a wind, fire, tongues, "drunkenness," praise, and prophecy. None of these was repeated except for tongues—and this occurred on each occasion where manifestations were described.

From this biblical analysis we conclude God has given speaking in tongues as a sign of receiving the Holy Spirit.

Note that we should not base beliefs on experiences, which can vary from person to person, and are also subject to interpretation. The Bible should be our guide.

IS THE EXPERIENCE FOR ALL CHRISTIANS?

Yes! There are two clear promises in the Bible:

> Repent and be baptized, every one of you…and you will receive the gift of the Holy Spirit. The promise is for you and your children and for all who are far off—for all whom the Lord our God will call.
>
> —ACTS 2:38–39

> …how much more will your Father in heaven give the Holy Spirit to those who ask him!
>
> —LUKE 11:9–13

God's desire is that every Christian should have this experience. Note that the onus is on us to ask.

How Do You Receive the Gift?

Ask God for the Holy Spirit, believing He will give it to you. You can pray on your own or have other Christians pray with you.

Begin praying with an expression of gratitude for sins forgiven and the gift of eternal life—words of thanks and praise. Then ask God for the gift of the Holy Spirit to give you power to serve Him better and be an effective witness.

As you are praying and receiving, expect to speak in tongues, and by faith begin to do so. You will find that very soon the sounds you make are not your own design—you are worshipping in a language you never learned. So you can conclude, along with the apostles long ago: these people "have received the Holy Spirit just as we have" (Acts 10:47).

What Then?

Having received this wonderful gift, you should put it to use. Speak in tongues daily, even hourly. Paul the Apostle explained that when we do this we "edify" ourselves (1 Cor. 14:4). He said, "I thank God that I speak in tongues more than all of you" (v. 18). He recognized clearly the benefits of speaking in tongues. It is your own personal prayer language. Read 1 Corinthians 14 for more of Paul's advice on its use.

The Holy Spirit baptism gives you power—use it as you have opportunity and as the Lord leads you. Expect to receive some of the nine gifts of the Holy Spirit (1 Cor. 12:7–10).

And marvel that you are one of millions of Christians worldwide who share the same experience and are working with all Christians to bring about God's purposes on Earth.

The baptism in the Holy Spirit is an extraordinary gift. To this must be added one more thing, even greater. Here it is.

Chapter 29
THE GREATEST LOVE OF ALL

A new command I give you: Love one another. As I
have loved you, so you must love one another.
—JOHN 13:34

If I give all I possess to the poor and give over my
body to hardship that I may boast, but do not have
love, I gain nothing.
—1 CORINTHIANS 13:3

EACH FORTNIGHT WE run a small group meeting in my home to worship, pray, study, and have fun. One night I spoke about the love of God. I was inspired by my son, Matthew, who had been very passionate about the following passage: "And I pray that you, being rooted and established in love, may have power, together with all the Lord's holy people, to grasp how wide and long and high and deep is the love of Christ, and to know this love that surpasses knowledge—that you may be filled to the measure of all the fullness of God" (Eph. 3:17–19).

Paul's prayer is obviously an important one—it is crucial that we receive *power* from God to *grasp the size* of God's love and also *know* God's love. Experiencing God's love is an oasis in our world of suffering, which can otherwise cloud your understanding of God's love and its outworking.

But having God's love is not just facts in your head. Certainly you can know facts about God's love in your head; but that passage opens the door to something different, an experience of God's love, and Matthew was praying hard for it to happen to him.

So I used this verse and several others and gave my talk, urging the group to pray that we might know that love. Next day I received an e-mail from one of the ladies in the group, Robyn Kyte, whom you read of earlier. She gave us the story of Mr. Black. Here is what she said:

Regarding last night's talk, here is something that happened to me many years ago.

One night God told me clearly that I was to go to India, so I spent the next year saving hard. Just before I went to the airport, the woman I was lodging with said she hoped God would bless me while I was away, because I had gone without so much to be able to make the trip. When I arrived in India, the beggars besieged me everywhere I went. I found them annoying, and quickly grew to dislike them.

In Calcutta, I met a German missionary, who I thought was the most saintly person I had ever met. His wife was back in Germany, as they had a baby boy who was very sick. In his first year the baby had several operations to save his life, and even whilst I was there underwent another one. The missionary wanted desperately to be with his wife and baby, but believed God wanted him in India, so he stayed, even though the boy could die at any time.

Calcutta lies in the state of West Bengal, which at that time was communist and imposed a number of restrictions on churches. But on Good Friday they were lifted, so they ran a six-hour church service from 9:00 a.m. to 3:00 p.m. A number of speakers took part, and I was invited to speak. The German missionary had also been asked to contribute and he went first. He stood up and began to cry, saying over and over: "If you only knew how much God loves you." That was his sermon; he said nothing else. One part of me was quite moved by it. But the other part of me rejected it, saying it was just emotionalism, and that part won.

That night I could not sleep. I tossed and turned, and the words of the missionary kept going round and round in my mind: "If you only knew how much God loves you." Finally, at 4:00 a.m., I knelt down beside the bed and said to God that I knew He was trying to tell me something, and I was willing to listen. Words are difficult to explain what happened next. God gave me a revelation of His love. It was vast. I felt that it was as big as the universe, yet knew at the same time that it was just a pinprick of the real size of God's love because

I could not cope with any more. I was greatly affected, sobbing for hours. Then I went out to the slum area in Calcutta, where so many beggars would besiege me. I walked all day through the slums, crying all the time as I saw them through entirely different eyes. They were people that God loved with that vast love.

That understanding of God's love continued throughout my time in India. Then I flew home, landing in Melbourne at 7:00 a.m. At the airport, I rang my agency to tell them I was back and available to work. They asked me to start that day in the city. In my lunch hour, as I was walking around the shops I felt the understanding of God's love just draining from me. There was so much materialism, so much of an emphasis on I, me, and myself. I recognized that such an emphasis on self effectively destroyed God's love at work in me.

I have always believed the reason why God gave me that revelation (and it has been the mainstay of my Christian walk) was because I made sacrifices to go to India. It was like He repaid me with His currency. What He gave me was of much greater value than the material things I went without. I think that's what happened with the German missionary. He made many more sacrifices than me by staying in India, and I believe God repaid him with a tremendous understanding of His love.

It's probably fair to say Robyn's experience of God's love equipped her to put up with the eccentricities of Mr. Black, whereas her six predecessors had quit. That was what was needed to get this knotted-up man free. I have known Robyn for more than three decades, and her patience and perseverance with Mr. Black is typical of the sacrificial love she demonstrates and which I have seen in her in many ways over that time.

I often try to imagine what the world would be like if everyone walked the same path as Robyn. What if every secretary treated her "Mr. Black" like that; what if every atheist decided to follow the evidence where it leads; what if every nurse could share Jesus with every wheelchair-bound patient; what if every scientist stopped to recognize God; what if every disabled child was given access to the

favors of God; what if everyone's wallet was lubricated by the generosity of God; what if every addict could grasp God's freedom; what
if every agnostic embraced God; and every Christian seized all the
favors God lavished on them, and devoted themselves to serving
God and His children?

Everyone in the world.

What would that be like?

NOTES

CHAPTER 1: THE ATHEIST PHILOSOPHER

1. Antony Flew with Roy Abraham Vargheses, *There Is a God* (New York: HarperOne, 2008), 52.
2. Ibid., 68.
3. Ibid., 12–13.
4. Ibid., 74.
5. Ibid., 112.
6. Ibid., 145.
7. Ibid., 154.
8. Ibid., 185.
9. Ibid., 157.
10. Ibid., 3.
11. Ibid., 75.
12. Thomas Nagel, *Mind and Cosmos: Why the Materialist Neo-Darwinian Conception of Nature Is Almost Certainly False* (New York: Oxford University Press, 2012), 128.
13. Ibid., 7.

CHAPTER 2: THE HONEST ATHEIST

1. David Catchpoole, "Atheists Credit the Gospel," *Creation* 32, no. 4 (2010): 48–49. Used by permission.

CHAPTER 3: THE ATHEIST AND THE SALVOS

1. Broadcast on BBC World Service, January 2, 2010, www.bbc.co.uk.
2. Catchpoole, "Atheists Credit the Gospel," 48–49.

CHAPTER 4: THE MARXIST ATHEIST

1. Peter McHugh (speech given at Federation Square, Melbourne, Australia, April 15, 2012). Used by permission.

CHAPTER 5: THE SCIENTISTS

1. Jerry Bergman, "From Skepticism to Faith in Christ: a Nobel Laureate's Journey," *Creation* 33, no. 2 (2011): 42–45. Used by permission.
2. Ibid.

3. Ibid.

4. Ibid.

5. Ibid.

6. Jonathan Sarfati, "Enzyme Expert Exposes Evolution's Error" *Creation* 32, no. 4 (2010): 42–44. Used by permission.

7. Ibid.

8. Ibid.

9. Philip Bell, "Expert Engineer Eschews 'Evolutionary Design'" *Creation* 32, no. 1 (2010): 35–37. Used by permission.

10. Ibid.

11. Ibid.

12. Ibid.

13. Ibid.

CHAPTER 6: DID JESUS EXIST?

1. Katharine Tait, *My Father Bertrand Russell* (New York: Harcourt Brace Jovanovich, 1975), 16.

2. Bertrand Russell quote can be found at http://thinkexist. com/quotation/i_would_never_die_for_my_beliefs_because_i_ might/10397.html (accessed February 22, 2013).

3. Norton Herbst, "Did Jesus Exist?" Exploring God, http://www. exploringgod.com/questions/did-jesus-exist (accessed February 19, 2013).

4. Josh McDowell, *The New Evidence that Demands a Verdict* (Nashville: Thomas Nelson, 1999).

5. Ibid.

6. Herbst, "Did Jesus Exist?"

7. Flavius Josephus, *Antiquities of the Jews*, 20.9.

8. Josephus, *Antiquities of the Jews*, 18.3.3, 63–64.

9. Herbst, "Did Jesus Exist?"

10. Ibid.

11. Publius Cornelius Tacitus, *Annals*, 15.44.

12. Herbst, "Did Jesus Exist?"

13. "Did Jesus Really Exist? Is There Any Historical Evidence of Jesus Christ?" Got Questions Ministries, http://www.gotquestions.org/ did-Jesus-exist.html (accessed February 19, 2013).

14. Ibid.

15. "Historicity of Jesus," *Wikipedia, The Free Encyclopedia*, http:// en.wikipedia.org/wiki/Historicity_of_Jesus (accessed February 19, 2013).

16. "Did Jesus Really Exist?" Got Questions Ministries.

17. Ibid.

18. "Historicity of Jesus," *Wikipedia.*

19. Michael Grant, *Jesus: An Historian's Review of the Gospels* (New York: Charles Scribner's Sons, 1977), 199–200.

CHAPTER 7: THE ALL-TIME NUMBER ONE BEST-SELLING BOOK

1. Paul Estabrooks, *Night of a Million Miracles* (Santa Ana, CA: Open Doors International, 2008).

CHAPTER 11: THE REBELLIOUS SON

1. Colton Wickramaratne, with Dishan Wickramaratne and Hal Donaldson, *My Adventure in Faith* (Springfield, MO: Onward Books, Inc., 2007), 998.

2. Ibid., 173.

3. Ibid., 220.

CHAPTER 13: THE GIVER

1. Tim Stafford, "Anatomy of a Giver," *Christianity Today* 41, no. 6 (1997), http://www.christianitytoday.com/ct/1997/may19/7t620a. html?start=2 (accessed February 19, 2013).

2. "How Christians Use Their Money…And Why," Highlights from a survey published by Christian Research (2005) and sponsored by Kingdom Bank (2006) http://www.stewardshipforum.org/pdfs/givingresearch.pdf (accessed February 19, 2013).

3. Ibid.

CHAPTER 16: GOD AND SEX

1. Herbert J. Miles, *Sexual Happiness in Marriage* (Grand Rapids, MI: Zondervan, 1987).

2. Martin Beckford, "Marriage More Stable Than Living Together, Office for National Statistics Finds," *The Telegraph*, March 26, 2010.

3. John Hayward, "The Secret of Sexual Satisfaction, Self-Fulfilment and a Strong Society," *Christian Today*, February 7, 2009, http://www.christiantoday.com/article/the.secret.of.sexual.satisfaction.self-fulfilment.and.a.strong.society/22445.htm (accessed February 22, 2013).

4. Mark Regnerus, "How Different Are the Adult Children of Parents Who Have Same-Sex Relationships? Findings from the New Family Structures Study" *Social Science Research* 41, no. 4 (2012): 752–770.

5. Ibid.
6. Ibid.
7. Ibid.

CHAPTER 18: THE BOY WHO WENT TO HEAVEN

1. Todd Burpo with Lynn Vincent, *Heaven Is for Real* (Nashville: Thomas Nelson, 2010), 56.
2. Ibid., xiv.
3. Ibid., xv.
4. Ibid., 81.
5. Ibid., 65.
6. Ibid., 67.
7. Ibid., 57.
8. Ibid., 59.
9. Ibid., 94.
10. Ibid., 122.
11. Ibid., 134.

CHAPTER 22: THE HINDU GURU

1. Rabi R. Maharaj and Dave Hunt, *Death of a Guru* (Eugene, OR: Harvest House Publishers, 1984), 59.
2. Ibid., 83.
3. Ibid., 96.
4. Ibid., 100.
5. Ibid., 108.
6. Ibid., 110.
7. Ibid., 116.
8. Ibid., 126.
9. Ibid., 129.
10. Ibid., 134.
11. Ibid.
12. Ibid., 197.

CHAPTER 23: THE MUSLIM

1. Elliot Spagat, "US Judge Agrees to Grant Asylum to Ex-Israeli Spy," *The Washington Post*, June 30, 2010.
2. Mosab Hassan Yousef, with Ron Brackin, *Son of Hamas* (Carol Stream, IL: Tyndale House, 2010), 63.
3. Ibid., 78.
4. Ibid., 19.

5. Ibid., 62.

6. Ibid., 120.

7. Ibid., 122.

8. Ibid., 127.

9. Ibid., 141.

10. Ibid., 178.

11. Ibid., 227.

12. Ibid., 244.

13. Ibid., 263.

14. Yousef, *Son of Hamas*, 249.

15. David Greenlee, *From the Straight Path to the Narrow Way* (Waynesboro, GA: Authentic Media, 2005), 167.

16. Ibid., 174.

17. J. Dudley Woodberry, Russell G. Shubin, and G. Marks, "Why Muslims Follow Jesus," *Christianity Today*, October 24, 2007, http://www.christianitytoday.com/ct/2007/october/42.80.html?start=2 (accessed March 6, 2013).

18. Greenlee, *From the Straight Path to the Narrow Way*, 165.

19. Greenlee, *From the Straight Path to the Narrow Way*, 15.

20. Ibid., 56.

21. Ibid., 104.

22. Ibid., 272.

CHAPTER 24: CHRISTIAN EVIL

1. Dr. Ken Chant, as quoted in *The Regal Standard*. Used by permission.

ABOUT THE AUTHOR

DENNIS PRINCE, AFTER working for six years as a lecturer in Civil Engineering, attended Bible College and in 1976 was co-planter of the thriving Kingston City Church in Melbourne, Australia. He and his musician wife, Nolene, then launched a Praise and Worship resource (Resource Christian Music), which was widely used around Australia and other countries for twenty-five years. Their rewrite of a 150-year-old vision of heaven by Marietta Davis—*Nine Days in Heaven*—has sold more than eighty thousand copies. Dennis has also published in Australia a book on the theology of praise and worship song lyrics, *Worship Is a Bowl of Noodles,* together with other teaching materials. Dennis and Nolene have three children, all married, and eleven grandchildren.

CONTACT THE AUTHOR

dennis@resource.com.au

BY THE SAME AUTHOR

NINE DAYS IN HEAVEN: A TRUE STORY
BY DENNIS AND NOLENE PRINCE

A rewrite in simple English of a remarkable vision of heaven and hell, experienced by twenty-five-year-old Marietta Davis, more than 150 years ago.

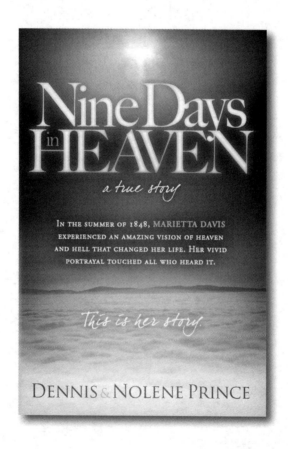

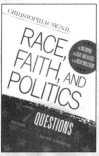